SECOND CHANCE

SECOND CHANCE

The United States and Indochina in the 1990s

FREDERICK Z. BROWN

Council on Foreign Relations Press
New York • London

COUNCIL ON FOREIGN RELATIONS BOOKS

Copyright © 1989 by the Council on Foreign Relations, Inc.
All rights reserved.
Printed in the United States of America

This book may not be reproduced, in whole or in part, in any form (beyond that copying permitted by Sections 107 and 108 of the U.S. Copyright Law and excerpts by reviewers for the public press), without written permission from the publishers. For information, write Publications Office, Council on Foreign Relations, 58 East 68th Street, New York, NY 10021.

Library of Congress Cataloguing-in-Publication Data

Brown, Frederick Z.
    Second chance.

    Includes bibliographical references.
        1. Indochina—Foreign relations—United States.
2. United States—Foreign relations—Indochina.
3. United States—Foreign relations—1945–.
I. Title.
DS546.5.U6B76   1989   327.730597   89–22074
ISBN 0-87609-069-2

89   90   91   92   93   94   PB   10   9   8   7   6   5   4   3   2   1

For Frances and Ellen

CONTENTS

FOREWORD

Alan D. Romberg

It was becoming increasingly clear in spring 1988 that the ten-year-old war in Cambodia was approaching a turning point. For a variety of reasons, most of them domestic but also reflecting growing confidence in the Cambodian regime it had installed in 1979, Vietnam was under pressure to withdraw its forces from the territory of its neighbor and had, in fact, pledged to do so by the end of 1990. However, in order to gain the benefits it sought in the international community, it was evident that Hanoi would need to go beyond merely ending its decade-long occupation and contribute to a political settlement satisfactory to all of the principal Cambodian and outside players.

Similarly, as great power relationships were evolving, the Cambodia question loomed as the main obstacle to achieving Soviet Party General Secretary Gorbachev's objective of normalizing relations with China. Thus, not only did Moscow encourage a negotiated settlement, but even on what was likely to be the most contentious issue, Soviet officials let it be known that the Kremlin was willing to see the brutal Khmer Rouge included in an interim structure in order to satisfy China that Beijing's interests were being protected.

The six member nations of the Association of Southeast Asian Nations (ASEAN), the principal backers of the noncommunist resistance led by Prince Norodom Sihanouk and former Prime Minister Son Sann, were actively promoting a peaceful resolution of the conflict, albeit with certain differences and tension among them. And, though it remained a second-order issue for the United States, it was obvious that Washington would have to reengage in Indochina, if not despite, then because of, the trauma of our previous role there.

It therefore seemed an opportune time for the Council on Foreign Relations to examine the conflict in Cambodia, the situation in Indochina as a whole, and U.S. interests and policy options in the area. Rita E. Hauser, a Council member, presented the Council with a generous grant to fund a series of studies on the resolution of regional conflicts, and it was decided that the proposed Indochina project should become the first of those studies.

We were fortunate that an expert on Indochina, Frederick Z. Brown, who had previously been a career foreign service officer and a staff member of the Senate Foreign Relations Committee, was available and shared the Council's view that a reexamination of U.S. policy toward Indochina was in order.

Finally, we were able to enlist the services of General John W. Vessey, Jr. (USA, Ret.), former chairman of the Joint Chiefs of Staff and currently the special presidential emissary for POW/MIA affairs, as chairman of the study group that we assembled to assist Fred Brown in his task. General Vessey acted, as did all other participants (listed in the Appendix), in a totally private capacity, and neither he nor anyone else in the study group should be held responsible for the contents of this book. Nonetheless, the contribution they made to the consideration of this complex set of issues was enormously helpful to the author.

The project also benefited at each stage from the expert guidance provided by the Council's then director of studies, Ambassador William H. Gleysteen, Jr.

Drawing on the generosity of the Rita E. Hauser Project on Regional Conflict, Bill Gleysteen, Fred Brown, and I traveled to the region for two and a half weeks in early 1989. We went to Thailand, Vietnam, Cambodia, and Japan, gathering firsthand information and drawing on insights of officials and private observers.

As this volume goes to press in late summer 1989, international attention is focused on the conference under way in Paris to help bring peace to the long-suffering Cambodian people.

Daily headlines reflect the ups and downs of the negotiations among the various Cambodian factions and their international sponsors and supporters. These tactical maneuvers may be of short-term interest, but the larger political, economic, security, and humanitarian concerns within Cambodia, and more broadly in Vietnam and the rest of Southeast Asia, are not at all transitory; they will be with us for many years to come. This book makes clear why Americans should be concerned; what it is we ought to be concerned about; and what policy options both interested citizens and government officials should keep in mind. America does have a second chance in Indochina—not to dominate or impose our solutions, but to help bring peace, stability, and (hopefully) prosperity to this troubled corner of the world.

Alan D. Romberg is senior fellow for Asia at the Council on Foreign Relations. Formerly a career foreign service officer, from 1981–85 he served as senior deputy assistant secretary of state for public affairs and deputy spokesman of the Department. He was director of the Department's Office of Japanese Affairs from 1978–80.

PREFACE

I am grateful to the Council on Foreign Relations for the opportunity to write this book, and to Rita E. Hauser for her generous contribution to the Council's Indochina study project.

The support and encouragement of the Council's president, Peter Tarnoff, and of William H. Gleysteen, Jr., Alan D. Romberg, and Dianne Schwartz of the Council's studies program were immensely helpful. Without the patience and sharp pens of Director of Publications David Kellogg and Managing Editor Suzanne Hooper, it would have been impossible to write, edit, and produce the final text in such a short time. I owe a special spiritual debt to my companions, Bill Gleysteen and Alan Romberg, on the trip to Vietnam, Cambodia, Thailand, and Japan in March 1989. Their wit and wisdom were invaluable during our field observations and interviews, as were their many cogent insights on all aspects of the book.

It was an honor to work with General John W. Vessey, Jr., whose leadership of the four Council study group sessions enlivened our discussions and spurred my own thinking about future relations with Vietnam.

The members of the study group (listed in the Appendix) and of the author's review group were not only generous with their time but exceptionally helpful in considering events in Indochina and U.S. policy from various perspectives. I appreciated the advice and aid of Bill Herod, director of the Indochina Project of the Fund for Peace, with whom I spent almost a month in Indochina in the summer of 1988 in the company of Dawn Calabia, then on the staff of the House Foreign Affairs Committee's Subcommittee on Asian and Pacific Affairs, Dalena Wright, legislative director for Representative Chester Atkins of Massachusetts, and William Nell, assistant director of the Aspen Institute Indochina Policy Forum. Some of the themes of this book had their genesis in that trip and were explored in the project's publication *Indochina Issues* of November 1988.

The Aspen Institute Indochina Policy Forum, chaired by Senator Dick Clark, has been an extraordinary venue for hours of thoughtful discussion and debate among Indochina buffs. The Forum helped shape my views on many aspects of the region's problems.

Evelyn Colbert, Paul H. Kreisberg, and Nayan Chanda made valuable suggestions on the entire book's organization and content. Robert A. Manning, Richard A. Melville, Naranhkiri Tith, Sichan Siv, Nguyen Manh Hung, Lewis M. Stern, Mark Carroll, Jane Carroll, Carl Harris, and Lionel A. Rosenblatt also read portions of it at various stages and commented helpfully. Donal R. Parks was an indispensable research assistant and the manipulator of an often user-unfriendly word processor.

I wish to thank Ambassador Trinh Xuan Lang, permanent representative of the Socialist Republic of Vietnam to the United Nations, and his staff for their assistance in making arrangements for my visits to Vietnam in 1988 and 1989.

Finally, I express my profound appreciation to Thomas L. Hughes, president of the Carnegie Endowment for International Peace. During fifteen months at the Endowment I had a rare opportunity to think and write about the United States and Southeast Asia, and to visit the region. The period of preparation and the creative environment offered by the Carnegie Endowment were essential ingredients in the writing of this book.

While recognizing the assistance and advice of all the individuals listed above, I alone am responsible for the interpretations and conclusions herein.

Frederick Z. Brown
Washington, D.C.

September 1989

WHAT'S IN A NAME?

The names and affiliations of the players in the Indochina drama can bewilder even seasoned observers of Southeast Asia. A few explanations about nomenclature are in order.

L'Indochine, "Indochina," the word conjures up the fragrance of frangipani, the whisper of *cyclo-pousse* along Saigon's lush boulevards, monks in saffron-colored robes scurrying through Angkor Wat, and the grand sweep of the Mekong River down from Laos and out to the South China Sea. Yet the term is misleading; a more precise but cumbersome reference would be "the countries of Vietnam, Cambodia, and Laos," since Indochina does not exist in any unified sense. The region contains three distinct countries with different languages, different cultures, different ethnic stocks, and a long history of mutual distrust and bitter antagonisms.

The Europeans, when they first arrived in that part of Southeast Asia, used "Indochina" to describe a region where the geography and influence of India from the west met that of China from the north. Originally, it included Thailand, Burma, and on some maps the Malay peninsula. The French, as they gradually solidified their grip on the three subregions of Vietnam (the north, center, and south, which the colons called Tonkin, Annam, and Cochinchine) and extended their reach into Cambodia and Laos, adopted "French Indochina" to describe this colonial domain. "Indochina" thus came to have a political meaning unrelated to the racial, geographical, and cultural factors that actually shape the region.[1]

The communists also viewed the region politically. From the early 1930s Ho Chi Minh's Indochinese Communist Party, created at the first Communist International, was the vehicle for revolution, primarily in Vietnam itself. Only in 1951 were three separate communist parties formed to mollify national sensibilities, but under firm Vietnamese control. According to General Vo Nguyen Giap, the architect of the communists' successful military strategy against the French, 1946–54, "Indochina is a strategic unit: a single theatre of operations, and here we have the mission to liberate all of Indochina."[2] In North Vietnam's fight against the United States and South Vietnam after 1954, the three countries were one battlefield—witness the Ho Chi Minh trail through Laos and the Cambodian sanctuaries to fight the "Vietnam War." The United States, in its military operations (especially from 1969 onward) adopted a similar single-theater strategy.

These days Hanoi avoids the term "Indochina" in order to blunt the charge of regional hegemony. But the idea of an Indochina under strong Vietnamese influence in one form or another is considered by many observers to be Hanoi's ultimate strategic objective in the region, if and when Vietnam is able to drag itself out of its current economic and social morass.

At the same time, the use of "Indochina" without qualification blurs an understanding of the region's residual nationalism and cultural definition. The Lao and especially the Cambodians—of all political stripes—resent being tossed into a common Indochinese pot. Thus while Vietnam continues to exert an inordinate influence over its weaker socialist sisters, this political connection is only part of the region's convoluted patterns. As Laos and Vietnam's protégé regime in Phnom Penh move in the direction of diversifying their international contacts, there are more nuances than ever.

Consequently, I speak of "Indochina" in this book with some misgivings. Let us count it a concession to convenience in discussing a situation that is already complex enough.

"Noncommunist Resistance" (NCR) is another unsatisfactory term. Again, I use it conventionally and because saying "the Sihanouk and Son Sann factions resisting the Vietnamese occupation" each time would be tiresome and distracting.

But NCR is misleading. When Vietnam gets out of Cambodia militarily, the NCR will be resisting a Cambodian government in Phnom Penh, which may or may not be Vietnam's puppet (the neat designation the State Department has used until recently and which Hanoi used during the war to describe the Diem and Thieu regimes).

NCR is negative. Surely Sihanouk and Son Sann's people must be for something as well as against the communists. "Pro-democracy forces" or "propluralist," even "freedom fighters" might be better, but what do those words mean in the current Cambodian political jungle? "Anticommunist Cambodians" would have the same semantic problem. And then we would have to explain why the NCR has been in a coalition with the most villainous "C" of all, the Khmer Rouge, since 1982.

Obviously we need snappy words like "Whig" and "Tory" to pin on each Cambodian faction. "Sihanoukists" is a partial solution—but where do Son Sann and a host of other noncommunists who are not wild about the monarchy fit in?

"Khmer" is the ethnic name for the people of Cambodia—hence the Khmer language, Khmer civilization, and of course the Khmer Empire of the eighth through the fourteenth centuries that created the many stunning monuments of the Siem Reap area, of which Angkor Wat is but the best known. "Khmer(s) Rouge(s)" (Red Khmer) is Prince Norodom Sihanouk's term from the French, since Pol Pot and many of his communist colleagues were educated in France. It is used throughout in the singular.

"Kampuchea" is the transliteration from Khmer language of the country's name. It is used by both the adherents of Pol Pot's Khmer Rouge faction—Democratic Kampuchea (DK)—and until recently the Phnom Penh regime—the People's Republic of Kampuchea (PRK). "Cambodia" is the English translation of the French "Le Cambodge." It is preferred by the two non-communist Khmer factions and has been used officially by the U.S. government since 1985. Many other countries and organizations, however, use Kampuchea. To confuse matters even more, the United States and the United Nations refer to the Coalition Government of Democratic Kampuchea (CGDK), since (as explained in subsequent chapters) the DK has legal title to Cambodia's UN seat, even though it is shared with the two noncommunist factions.

A final confusion is that the People's Republic of Kampuchea, in May 1989, rechristened itself the "State of Cambodia" (SOC) to deemphasize its Marxist character and identify with the country's cultural heritage.

C H I N A

Malipo
Pingguo
Nanning
Ha Giang
Cao Bang
Lao Chau
Pingxiang
Phongsali
Thai Nguyen
Hanoi
Hong Gai
Nam Dinh
Gulf of Tonkin
HAINAN DAO
Louangphrabang
Ban Ban
Thanh Hoa
Cua Rao
Chiang Rai
Muang Pak San
Vinh
Ha Tinh
Vientiane
Nong Khai
Ron
Nakhon Phanom
Dong Hoi
Sakon Nakhon
LAOS
Khon Kaen
Savannakhét
Hue
Roi Et
Da Nang
Saravan
Ubon Ratchathani
Pakxé
T H A I L A N D
Quang Ngai
Surin
Champasak
Attapeu
Kontum
Pleiku
VIETNAM
Bangkok
Sisŏphŏn
Stœng Trêng
Lumphat
Siĕmréab
Bătdâmbâng
CAMBODIA
Buon Me Thuot
Pôŭthĭsăt
TONLE SAP
Krâchéh
Nha Trang
Kâmpóng Chhnăng
Cham Ranh
Krŏng Kaôh Kŏng
Phnom Penh
Prey Vêng
Da Lat
Takêv
Ta Ninh
Phan Thiet
Kâmpóng Saôm
Ho Chi Minh City
Vung Tau
Rach Gia
Can Tho
Vinh Long
Ca Mau
Gulf of Thailand

BURMA

MEKONG
SALWEEN
MAI NAM NAN
MEKONG
KE KONG
MEKONG

South China Sea

INDOCHINA

0   100   200   300 M.

0   100   200   300 K.

Ascherl

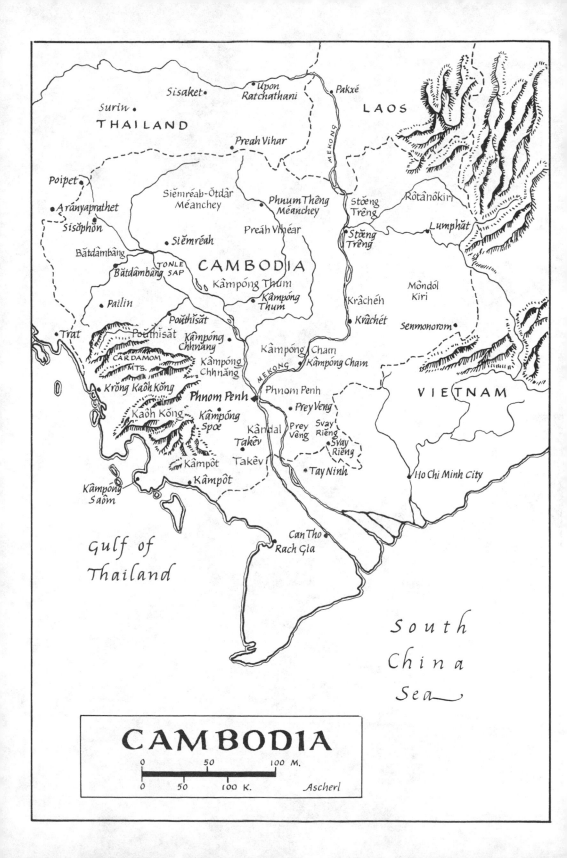

1

INTRODUCTION: VIETNAM AGAIN?

America became involved in Indochina one blustery day in October 1776 when Benjamin Franklin set sail from Philadelphia to become the colonies' ambassador-plenipotentiary to the court of Louis XVI in Paris. This early Franco-American relationship begat a Eurocentrist American foreign policy that ultimately led to the decision taken by the Truman administration in 1946 to support reimposition of France's imperial hold on Indochina, despite misgivings expressed by President Franklin Roosevelt not long before his death. The practical effect was to deny Vietnamese aspirations for independence and to make inevitable the nine-year war that followed, in which the United States was France's major supporter.

Other prominent reasons contributed to our involvement in Indochina after 1954. The Chinese communists' victory on the mainland in 1949 and the 1950 Sino-Soviet Treaty of Friendship, Alliance, and Mutual Assistance caused the United States grave concern with the threat of a monolithic Sino-Soviet expansion throughout Asia. The Korean War heightened this fear. Vietnam became our "Asian Berlin," a test of American steadfastness against world communism. But it was the French connection that, many years before, set in motion the process leading to the United States' taking charge of the Vietnam War in 1963–65, with all that followed.[1]

It is fashionable these days to speak of the 21st century as the "century of the Pacific." In truth, East Asia and the Pacific have been strategically important to the United States for most of the present century. In the bloody Pacific campaigns of World War II, the United States defended what it defined as its vital national interests in the region. Around the globe in the succeeding years, only in East Asia—in Korea and in Indochina—did the United

1

States commit ground forces to fight in an overseas military conflict.

East Asia has become the most dynamic region in the world economically. With Europe and the Middle East, it is a critical crossroads for U.S. interests. The Soviet Union's vigorous East Asia and Pacific diplomatic offensive throughout the region, Japan's rise as an economic power, the growing frictions in U.S.–Japan relations, the turmoil in China, the continuing tensions on the Korean peninsula—these are but the most obvious indicators of a "Pacific Century" that holds complex problems as well as opportunities for the United States.

As for Indochina, one can only view what happened there not so long ago with a sense of disbelief. How did we get involved so deeply in that remote corner of the world? How could a venture with such good intentions end so tragically for us and the Indochinese we were trying to help?

Looking back, it is hard to realize that only 21 years ago the United States was trapped in a military involvement that eventually took 58,000 American lives. The communist Tet offensive in February 1968 symbolized the frustration, and to many Americans the folly, of the Vietnam quagmire. Admitting personal defeat, Lyndon Johnson declined to run again for the presidency and became a casualty of the domestic turmoil of the 1960s in which Vietnam and civil rights were central elements.

During the early 1970s, Indochina dominated the deliberations of the Senate Foreign Relations Committee as the country tried to extricate itself from the entanglement. Within the Congress, in the media, and among Americans of all political persuasions, American foreign policy—indeed many aspects of our value system—were examined exhaustively in the light of Vietnam's lessons. The repercussions went well beyond Indochina. The bipartisan consensus that was the basis for foreign policy under Presidents Truman and Eisenhower and that extended into the Kennedy era was severely shaken. The Watergate scandal and Richard Nixon's forced resignation were the direct result of the president's anxiety over the antiwar movement. Within a few months, these events and the congressional elections of 1974

2

ended U.S. support for the Thieu government in South Vietnam and the Lon Nol government in Cambodia. John F. Kennedy's inaugural call to go anywhere and pay any price in support of freedom no longer rang true with either the Congress or the American public.

Today the effects of the Vietnam experience are felt throughout our contemporary life—in the drug culture originating in that earlier period, in the ruptured post–World War II premise about our role in the world, and in the altered relationship between the executive and legislative branches of government in making and managing foreign policy.

In foreign affairs, the crises of the moment invariably preempt well-considered policy. Indochina for most Americans is not a crisis but a humiliation better forgotten. It is thus not surprising that, except for a flurry of enthusiasm for normalization with Vietnam in the early Carter years, three U.S. administrations since 1975 have assigned Indochina low priority. For policymakers, Southeast Asia has sunk to a third-rank priority on the global agenda, and Indochina has become almost invisible. Only since about 1988 have prospects for a settlement in Cambodia and the gruesome possibility of a return to power of the Khmer Rouge excited interest in Washington. At the same time, leaders from both political parties are apprehensive over reinvolvement, however slight, in the affairs of Indochina. The wounds are still fresh and the domestic political risk still evident.

The American people have been ambivalent about Indochina, when they have cared to think about it. They have been caught between curiosity about what went wrong and a counterimpulse to block out the whole "mess." Absorbed in the war's drama and corrosive social impact, Americans have preferred to view the war through the cinema prisms of "Platoon" and "Full Metal Jacket" or TV soap operas like "Tour of Duty" and "China Beach" (Vietnam's "M*A*S*H"). An avalanche of war novels about American soldiers in "Nam" have come to press. In most of these films and novels Vietnam becomes a fictional country where Vietnamese rarely appear except as targets, and this says a good deal about our misconceptions of what the war was all about.[2]

This attitude appears to be changing. Although Indochina still ranks well down in the administration's foreign policy priorities, a more comprehensive process of examination is under way in the American public. The reactive blocking out of Vietnam shows signs of giving way to a more mature attitude and to a desire to understand the reasons for our past involvement and prospects for the future. The profusion of college courses on the war and serious documentaries on Vietnam and Cambodia indicate as much. The process is slow; no one can predict what revisions of reality and belief will occur along the way.

The principal theme of this book is that a preoccupation with the trauma of an involvement a generation ago should not obscure today's realities or preclude thoughtful consideration of a new relationship with the three countries of Indochina, and particularly with Vietnam, in the broader regional context of Southeast Asia. Life still goes on in Indochina despite the events of 1975. Saigon did not "fall," it became Ho Chi Minh City. Three million Vietnamese live there—and they still call it Saigon.

A second theme is Cambodia. *Les etats sont les monstres cruels et froids* (loosely translated from the French, "States are monsters who are cruel and indifferent"), Prince Norodom Sihanouk is fond of saying about a Cambodia caught over the centuries in the machinations of more powerful neighbors. This book is about the policies of nations that throughout Indochina's history, and especially with regard to Cambodia, have often been cruel and indifferent to the fate of the Khmer people.

Third, the book is about American attitudes, because public attitudes shape public policy. Nowhere, surely, has this been more apparent than in the saga of our involvement in Indochina. In the final chapter, I argue for a rechanneling of American attitudes from the rejection and bitterness prevailing since 1975—the "Vietnam syndrome"—in a more constructive direction. Pragmatic foreign policy interests would be well served by such a change.

In his 1989 inaugural address President Bush said, " . . . surely the statute of limitations has been reached. This is a fact: The final lesson of Vietnam is that no great nation can long afford to be sundered by a memory." A redirection of our attitudes might help heal the psychological wounds of the Vietnam War that, despite President Bush's brave words, are still so profoundly felt. Putting an end to the war within us, as the president has suggested, possesses a value of its own.

The book is neither a history of Indochina since 1975 nor a balanced analysis of all aspects of the U.S. relationship with the Association of Southeast Asian Nations (ASEAN) and its six member countries. The important issues of trade, intellectual property rights, drugs, economic development, nuclear weapons, human rights, and a host of lesser matters are treated briefly, if at all. A comprehensive discussion of Indochinese refugees—the history of the problem, the accomplishments of ASEAN and the international community, and the dilemmas that remain unsolved—would demand a work several times this length.

With the focus upon Cambodia and Vietnam, Laos is addressed only in passing, a decision I have taken deliberately because Laos, in my view, is not a policy area in need of special attention. The United States never broke diplomatic relations with the country (which became the Lao People's Democratic Republic, LPDR, in December 1975), and our relationship has developed along a path different in quality and depth from the fragmentary contacts we have had with Laos' two Indochina colleagues.

In Indochina affairs, Laos is dwarfed in importance because of its size (the population of Vietnam is 65 million versus Laos' 3.5 million) and because of the gravity of the Cambodia issue. This does not mean that the U.S.–Laos relationship is inconsequential, only that there are limits to what can be expected from it, and these limits have been fairly well staked out. U.S. policy vis-à-vis Laos is about where it should be under current circumstances.

This book addresses U.S. policy toward only one subregion of East Asia and the Pacific, Indochina, and the two dominant issues there: negotiating a solution to the Cambodia problem, and building a new relationship with Vietnam. On these issues,

U.S. policy in recent years has deliberately followed the lead of others. While this was appropriate in the years immediately following 1975, the book suggests that administrations in recent years have been unimaginative and slow to respond to the challenges of a changing situation.

Indochina is not the center of the American foreign policy universe, nor is it likely ever again to dominate our national psyche as it did in the 1960s and early 1970s. Our goals today in Indochina are vastly different from what they were in the 1950s—and France has become a leader in the international initiative to solve the Cambodia problem. There are limits to what the United States can do to influence the course of events in East Asia and certainly in Indochina. Although not without economic, political, and military power, we are no longer the prime determinant—if we ever were—of events in the region.

Far from advocating a replay of an earlier crusade, this book suggests that the United States, in the multipolarity of the 1990s, nonetheless has the capability to influence the evolution of a new Indochina in a healthy direction, a direction which could benefit not only the peoples of the area but U.S. national interests as well. In this sense, the United States has a second chance in Indochina.

2

U.S. INTERESTS IN INDOCHINA

Looking back, one is struck by how dramatically the situation in Southeast Asia has changed since the "fall of Saigon." The evolution of U.S. policy toward the region actually started well before the cataclysmic events of April 1975.

The Sino-Soviet rift beginning in the late 1950s paved the way for the growth of a broad relationship between China and the United States in the 1970s and created a new global strategic environment for American policy. The evolution of Chinese domestic and foreign policies away from Maoism and a more realistic perception in U.S. foreign policy of the Sino-Soviet bloc all but put an end to calls for Kennedy-type interventions. (Though the spring 1989 events in China cast serious doubt on just how profound that evolution has been in domestic terms, the impact on Chinese foreign policy is not yet clear.) The United States was no longer seen, and no longer saw itself, as the guardian angel of a region vulnerable to conquest by a monolithic communist empire, a threat taken almost for granted in the United States three decades ago. The noncommunist countries of the Association of Southeast Asian Nations matured and prospered.* Collectively, they emerged as a valuable asset to the United States, thanks in no small part to their spirit of self-reliance and independence. Our former adversaries in Vietnam were mired in economic and social decay. For Americans, Vietnam was no longer our problem except as the aggressor in Cambodia; that was mainly ASEAN's problem to manage, and ASEAN was willing to take it on.

All these trends, with the obvious exception of the Cambodia tragedy, have yielded geopolitical gains for the United

* The members of ASEAN are Thailand, Malaysia, Singapore, Indonesia, the Philippines, and Brunei, which joined in 1984.

States. Since the end of the Vietnam War, U.S. policy has chosen to focus on issues beyond Indochina: the relationship with ASEAN; regional economic development and trade; and rapprochement with China as it touches the region. But with the Cambodia issue submerged into the regional context, the United States has formulated no comprehensive strategy of its own toward Indochina since 1975. Events have unfolded without great planning on our part, and they can be grouped within three periods:

- the two years of shock and retrenchment under the Ford administration;

- the brief effort to normalize relations with Vietnam during the first half of the Carter administration; and

- the years of American low profile and deference to ASEAN and China beginning with the Vietnamese invasion of Cambodia in late 1978 and extending to the present.

The thrust of Washington's policy can be summed up in Frank Lloyd Wright's architectural principle that less is more. Most observers here and in Southeast Asia have judged it appropriate to the post-Vietnam period and remarkably successful in accomplishing our rather circumscribed objectives. Improvement of bilateral relations with individual Southeast Asian countries and with ASEAN are often cited as success stories of American foreign policy since 1975.

Today such claims of success, if unexamined, would smack of complacency. Developments on the world scene and in Southeast Asia, particularly from 1986 onward, raise questions about the continued appropriateness of several aspects of U.S. policy. It is worth asking if the comfortable assumptions of the last decade and a half are still valid. Has the United States fully understood the ramifications of changes taking place not only within ASEAN but also with regard to Vietnam and to the Soviet role in the region? Have we taken into account the impact of Soviet President Mikhail Gorbachev's announced intention to make the Soviet Union a full-fledged player—economically and politically, as well as militarily—in Asia and the Pacific?

These questions lead to the main theme of this book: Why should the United States care much about what happens in Indochina, that sad part of the world which used to be so important to us but which, strangely, now seems irrelevant?

Indochina does not exist in isolation but alongside some of our best friends in Asia. In computing the bottom line of U.S. political and economic interests, and in devising a rational Indochina strategy, our collective relationships with the other countries of Southeast Asia loom larger than any we are likely to develop with the three Indochina states in the next generation. But there does not have to be an "either-or" choice. If we act carefully, continued close ties with our current friends elsewhere in East Asia are not incompatible with a new relationship with Indochina. Indeed, they should be complementary.

The major East Asian powers care about and are already involved in Indochina: politically and militarily in the case of China, economically in the case of Japan, and strategically in a growing number of ways in the case of the Soviet Union. Arguably, the Cold War may be abating; more likely it is changing venue and style. In any event, Gorbachev's smile does not remove the necessity of a strong (if perhaps modified) U.S. military presence in East Asia and the Pacific. Politically and economically, there can be no question of the need for a continued major, active U.S. role—this is at the heart of the region's stability.

The United States cannot dictate the course of events in Indochina, even if it wished to do so, but it should not by default cede preponderant influence there to the Soviet Union and China. With modest political and economic investment, and with higher policy priority assigned by the administration, the United States can improve its stature in Southeast Asia and more broadly in the rest of Asia.

Vietnam, with its 65 million people, counts now; by the year 2000, it will weigh heavily in regional affairs. One does not have to admire the

9

current government in Hanoi or its policies to admit that it exists. As leadership changes already under way demonstrate, the Vietnamese leaders are not immortal nor, it would seem, are they totally blind to their failures. We should position ourselves now to influence not only the evolving policies of the current leadership, but also a rising generation of Vietnamese who may come to see the world somewhat differently. Again, while American influence is modest, we and ASEAN can help shape the evolution of Vietnam's role in the region in the next decades.

U.S. interests would benefit if Vietnam ceased being a disruptive force and moved away from Marxism-Leninism and from its intimate ties to the Soviet Union. We should do what is possible to promote such change. Even if elimination of Soviet influence in Indochina is an impractical goal, loosening Soviet-Vietnamese ties is not, and that, plus the eventual removal of Soviet military bases from Vietnam, should be a long-term objective of U.S. policy. Put more positively, it is not too audacious to imagine a future Vietnam that has close relations with the Soviet Union, yet as a newly industrializing economy (NIE) can also maintain good relations with the capitalist world. An imaginative and resourceful foreign policy should enable the United States to advance its interests in this environment.

As for "normalization," the United States was at war with half of Vietnam for the first 20 years of that country's independence from France (1954–73). There has been mutual hostility for an even longer period. In this context it is difficult to know what "normal" really means. One thing is certain: normalization is a process, not a fixed destination. An intelligent relationship will take years to build even with the best of intentions on both sides. But as soon as political conditions permit, the process should begin.

Indochina offers economic opportunities. Our future commerce with Vietnam is not going to reverse the U.S. international trade imbalance. The Vietnamese economy is a mess and opportunities are limited now, but the country has rich resources and a talented people who, had they the means, are ready to do business. If and when reforms in dogma and in practice take hold, there will be attractive trade opportunities for foreigners. At least the hundreds of Japanese, Korean, Taiwan, and ASEAN (particularly Thai and Singaporean) business executives already streaming into Ho Chi Minh City are banking on this. Why should the United States leave the Indochina markets to Japan and the "young tigers" of Asia?

Of most immediate concern, the United States has an interest in an equitable settlement in Cambodia. The decade-long Cambodia stalemate is moving toward some sort of solution, with or without the United States. Given our relationship with the rest of Southeast Asia, it is in the U.S. interest to remove Cambodia as a source of instability, and in that sense we stand to gain from a political settlement.

Stating this addresses only half the question. A settlement that suits the geopolitical requirements of the outside powers may not do justice to the aspirations of the Cambodian people and their ultimate fate. The goals of U.S. policy are withdrawal of all Vietnamese military forces; the nonreturn of the Khmer Rouge to power; a political settlement that permits the Cambodian people to choose their own form of government; and ultimately a Cambodia that is independent, neutral, nonaligned, and protected by international guarantees from outside interference.

All this may be a marvelous abstraction. In cold reality, the United States must decide how much it really wants an equitable settlement for the Cambodians, and start by asking itself tough questions:

- How deeply are we prepared to become involved in the process of negotiations and the search for a settlement?

- What commitments are we prepared to make to an international effort to guarantee the settlement and to reconstruct the country?

- How do we define "democracy" in the context of a country which has never enjoyed it, has known only one-party rule or an authoritarian (sometimes benevolent) "God-king," and has among its Southeast Asian neighbors only a few with democratic pretensions?

- What can we realistically hope to achieve in Cambodia and what are the tools at our disposal?

We have heard much anguish from some sectors of the administration, Congress, and the public over preventing the Khmer Rouge from returning to power, and also the need for pluralism in a future Cambodia. The prevailing view among Washington policymakers, however, seems to be that, in the world of thawing superpower relations and shrinking budgets, Indochina is of relatively minor importance in the firmament of U.S. foreign policy interests and that we should make minimum political and material investment there, even to help the long-suffering Cambodians.

The United States should be capable of following a minimalist, noninterventionist strategy that is nonetheless more active and responsive to the challenges of a new situation in Cambodia. Such a policy would emphasize multilateral diplomacy, international cooperation, and the creative use of tools already at our disposal. Among the more important mechanisms are:

- close relations not only with ASEAN but with Japan, which has both an interest in Indochina and capital to invest there;

- a special intimacy with Thailand;

- a Vietnam that needs the benefits of relations with the United States;

- the triangular relationship with China and the Soviet Union that permits us to influence events through the Cambodia conflict's great power patrons;

- Cambodian-Americans with expertise and money, some of whom will risk direct involvement in a settlement through economic investment and a physical presence; and

- a skilled, experienced, highly motivated private voluntary agency community eager to pitch in.

It is perhaps implicit that the neat formula of letting ASEAN take the lead on Cambodia, although still important, is insufficient to guide U.S. policy. Moreover, the ground is shifting within the Association and in its external relations, in large measure because the prospect of a Cambodia settlement has already broken the logjam in Indochina. The premise of a unified ASEAN policy on Cambodia is no longer valid. Thailand will quickly establish trade links with Cambodia, and deepen those already established with Vietnam. In Thai Prime Minister Chatichai's words, ASEAN wants Indochina to become "a marketplace instead of a battlefield." Hanoi is clearly moving in this direction, but, as yet, what implications commerce may hold as the magic potion for Indochina's political ills are not clear. Much depends on the timing of these changes and on the conditions set for Vietnam's gradual inclusion in ASEAN's trading patterns.

The Soviet Union has become a significant factor in Southeast Asia. Moscow has tended to view its strategic interests in Southeast Asia in the context of its relationships with China and the United States. The American defeat in Indochina presented an extraordinary opportunity to take advantage of the historical antagonism between China and Vietnam. After supplanting China as North Vietnam's major supporter during the war, particularly in high-technology items such as surface-to-air missiles, the Soviets cemented the relationship with massive economic and military assistance and stood behind Vietnam when it invaded Cambodia. Since 1975 Vietnam has become almost totally dependent on the Soviet Union, and this dependence has created a fresh geopolitical dimension for the USSR in Indochina.

Until recently, the Soviets had little interest in or capability of pursuing fruitful relations with the noncommunist countries of Southeast Asia.* In a competitive sense, U.S. economic and

* An exception was the costly Indonesia fiasco in the early 1960s when the Soviets attempted, unsuccessfully, to purchase goodwill through huge amounts of military assistance to the Sukarno regime.

political clout plus its prestige and military presence in the Pacific as a result of World War II were overwhelming. Even without these factors, the ingrained suspicion of communist intentions, the free market orientation of the region's economies, and the Soviets' unattractiveness as a trading partner combined to create an objective reality distinctly unfavorable to Soviet activities.

Enter Mikhail Gorbachev, and exit Soviet reticence. The general secretary's pronouncements at Vladivostok, in July 1986, and at Krasnoyarsk, in September 1988, and his skillful use of the Southeast Asia media to project his message (his July 1987 interview with the Indonesian paper *Merdeka* on arms control, for example) leave no doubt of Gorbachev's intention to establish the Soviet Union as an Asia-Pacific power and to extend Soviet interests well beyond Indochina. By assigning sophisticated, activist Asian specialists to ASEAN and Pacific capitals to replace some of the stereotypical Soviet Cold Warriors, Gorbachev has sought to improve bilateral relations with all the noncommunist countries of the region and with the Association.

Soviet goals are to dilute U.S. and Chinese influence in the region, to project the image of a peaceful, enlightened superpower, and where possible to stimulate trade of benefit to the Soviet economy. Thus far the results have not been spectacular. The Soviets still have few economic and commercial resources; there is widespread skepticism regarding their intentions; and specifics on what they are actually proposing to enhance prospects for peace are sparse and clouded in ambiguity. But the Soviet rapprochement with China, reductions of defense expenditures, removal of SS-20s aimed at Asian targets, decreases in the number of planes and ships deployed in the Far East, and the perception of pressure on Hanoi to quit Cambodia all evidence Moscow's new "reasonable" posture. The Soviet Union is trying much harder to be an important player in a region where until relatively recently it has been of negligible importance, and the United States is being challenged on geographic and diplomatic turf it liked to think was its own.[1] Still, the Soviets' strength today in Southeast Asia derives, as in the past, from the relationship

14

with Vietnam, not from significant political or economic strides elsewhere.

Indochina is only one part of this mosaic of Soviet activity, and it happens to be the geographic location where the United States has least direct capability at this time. But if the United States is to remain a player in the power games of East Asia, it can ill afford to treat any subregion as a diseased appendage better kept under quarantine. If only to balance the Soviet Union, we should establish a working, even positive relationship with Vietnam that takes into account our existing ties with Southeast Asia. This should be done prudently as soon as conditions in Cambodia permit.

Gorbachev's initiatives have kept Washington in a largely defensive mode. The problem, however, goes beyond the Soviets' flashy pitch. Some of our friends in Southeast Asia believe that the United States is not fully aware of the speed and significance of geopolitical changes in the region, and that it consequently is reluctant to contemplate strategic questions relating to Indochina, such as a future relationship with Vietnam. Whether intended or not, this seemingly aloof attitude toward Vietnam as part of the broader picture in Southeast Asia appears to signal friends and adversaries alike that the Soviet Union and China are welcome to negotiate the future of Indochina with only casual concern for what the United States might think.

The current move toward a political settlement in Cambodia opens up the opportunity for a more thoughtful, participatory American policy not only on the immediate issues in that fast-changing scene, but also more in keeping with our long-term obligations and interests in the region. The United States does not have to "take the lead" in order to be more active in a constructive fashion, which is what our friends in the region—and, oddly enough, some who are not considered our friends—would like to see happen.

At the July 1989 ASEAN postministerial conference in Brunei, the Bush administration confirmed that the United States would play a more active role in the resolution of the Cambodia problem in the July-August international conference and in follow-up measures. How far the administration would go and whether it could come up with a sustained program for other aspects of Indochina, including building a new relationship with Hanoi once the Vietnamese got out of Cambodia, remained problematical.

The evolution of U.S. relations with Eastern Europe in the late 1980s holds direct relevance for Indochina. If the United States could reach out to the communist regimes of Poland and Hungary—and applaud their leaders for having admitted the bankruptcy of Marxism-Leninism—then similar circumstances in Southeast Asia clearly offer opportunities to improve U.S. relations with Vietnam and a new regime in Cambodia, which will include a communist faction.

Finally, the crushing of the democracy movement in China and the apparent return to political practices of a past era may call for renewed scrutiny of China's intentions in Southeast Asia. With regard to the external implications of recent events, two issues are pending: first, China's willingness to reduce and eventually stop aid to the Khmer Rouge and then perhaps accept their top leaders in exile when Vietnamese forces leave Cambodia; and second, China's normalization of relations with Vietnam, already under way after more than a decade of outright hostility. Moreover, a third issue could conceivably arise again from history—a rebirth of Chinese support for insurgencies in Southeast Asia or other forms of destabilizing measures. Any objective cost-benefit analysis would seem to argue against such actions by Beijing, but the possibility of something quite unexpected during the current period of internal political realignment cannot be ruled out.

The uncertainty of the current situation in China makes it all the more important to develop a dialogue with Vietnam on regional issues. Indonesia has for some time viewed Vietnam as a potential bulwark against an unpredictable China. The future politics of the region may make for some strange bedfellows. This is not to suggest a Vietnamese-American *entente cordiale* or to forecast Chinese aggression in the region. Obviously, the United States has a paramount interest in rebuilding a constructive relationship with China, and that track must be energetically pushed as conditions permit. It is only to point out that the geopolitical alignments in the Southeast Asian regional context have become even more complicated in the wake of recent events in the People's Republic of China (PRC). A few years hence, as these permutations develop, Vietnam may assume considerably greater importance for the United States, and certainly for our friends in the region.

3

AFTER THE FALL

Hanoi's victory in April 1975 drastically modified the power balance in Southeast Asia. The helicopter lift-off from the roof of the U.S. embassy in Saigon astounded and embarrassed America's friends everywhere. Cambodia had fallen to the Khmer Rouge two weeks earlier. In Laos, the Pathet Lao seized full power in August, thus completing the destruction of all of the Indochina governments or coalition arrangements supported by the United States for more than two decades.

ASEAN now faced a victorious North Vietnam with an army of one million men. On its eastern border Thailand saw a Cambodia under control of the brutal, unpredictable Khmer Rouge of Pol Pot. In this uncertain situation, the noncommunist countries of the region had reason to doubt the constancy and reliability of the United States. The dismantlement of the Southeast Asia Treaty Organization (SEATO), the most visible U.S. commitment to the security of the region but long suspected of being a "paper tiger," was proposed in July 1975 and took effect in 1977. A civilian government in Thailand asked for the removal of what had become a very large U.S. military presence, reinforcing the image of the United States wounded and in retreat.

For the Ford administration, restoration of confidence in the United States as a reliable ally, not only in Southeast Asia but globally as well, became the number one priority. The Middle East, the commitment to NATO, and the uneasy relationship with the Soviet Union—each of these vital areas had felt the impact of Indochina. The reestablishment of U.S. credibility thus became imperative.

Credibility had by 1969 already become the dominant consideration in continuing support for the U.S.–backed Republic of Vietnam (RVN). The policy of "Vietnamization," the military operations such as the 1970 Cambodia incursion, and the thrust of the protracted peace negotiations conducted by National Security Adviser Henry Kissinger and senior Politburo member Le Duc Tho had all been designed to facilitate, if possible, a graceful American exit from the Indochina involvement with its superpower credibility intact and "peace with honor."

As the RVN was disintegrating in March 1975, Assistant Secretary of State for East Asian and Pacific Affairs Philip Habib stated bluntly, "We no longer see the security of the United States as directly, immediately at issue. Nevertheless, it remains true that failure to sustain our purposes in Indochina would have a corrosive effect on our ability to conduct effective diplomacy worldwide."[1] President Ford in his first press conference after the Saigon embassy evacuation declared, "I think the lessons of the past in Vietnam have already been learned . . . and we should have our focus on the future. As far as I am concerned, that is where we will concentrate."[2]

The *Mayaguez* incident a week later, when the United States took military action to rescue the 39 crew members of an American ship seized by the Khmer Rouge, was portrayed by some officials as an opportunity to prove that the United States was still a power to be reckoned with. The cost was 18 marines killed or missing, and 50 wounded, and an adverse impact on our relations with Thailand, from whose territory the U.S. operation was launched.[3]

One notable diplomatic effort to reassure American friends in Asia was President Ford's visit in December 1975 to Japan, the PRC, Indonesia, and the Philippines after which a six-point Pacific Doctrine was put forward. The fourth point (after credibility, Japan, and China) was our "continuing stake in stability and security in Southeast Asia."[4]

No broad plan for a future U.S. role in Southeast Asia emerged during the two years after the Indochina disaster. The desire to put Vietnam behind us seemed to extend to all of Southeast Asia, despite the fact that the Vietnam War had been fought in large measure to protect our friends from aggression that Washington thought would certainly come without deep American involvement. The Southeast Asians had, in fact, used the time of the U.S. involvement in Vietnam to strengthen their political systems and to develop burgeoning national economies.

The U.S. disengagement of the 1975–76 period also spurred ASEAN into taking even greater responsibility for its own destiny.

The Southeast Asia "dominoes" did not fall in the years after the U.S. departure. The countries survived because of their own strength and despite the American departure from the battlefield. When it took on the defense of Southeast Asia in the 1950s, it is fair to say the United States did not plan it precisely that way, although our hope was that somehow behind our protective wall noncommunist countries would become stronger and more stable—and in the Guam Doctrine President Nixon announced they had.[5] The U.S. contribution to the economic development of the region by the infusion of capital and technology during the war years (and by providing a market for the products of these developing countries) may have been more significant than anything we did militarily.

In the aftermath of the traumatic events of early 1975, the Ford administration addressed the question of normalization of relations with Vietnam guardedly. In June, Secretary Kissinger, acknowledging that "new regimes have come to power in Asia in the last few months," said that the United States was "prepared to look to the future" but would be influenced by how these regimes acted toward their neighbors as well as toward the United States.[6] By the end of the Ford administration this position remained substantially the same, but some particulars had been added. In September 1976, Assistant Secretary of State Arthur Hummel reiterated that the United States still looked to the future, not the past, but specified that "for us the most serious single obstacle in proceeding toward normalization is the refusal of Hanoi to give us a full accounting of those missing in action [MIA]."* Regarding provision of postwar reconstruction

* The Woodcock Commission report (see page 22 below) stated that "there is no evidence to indicate that any American POWs from the Indochina conflict remain alive" (*Department of State Bulletin, No. 76*, April 18, 1977, p. 373, quoting a White House press release dated March 23, 1977). The term "MIA" was used during the years immediately following the war. Refusing to foreclose the possibility that live Americans might still be held against their will, however, the Reagan administration adopted the acronym "POW/MIA."

assistance to Vietnam as part of the Kissinger–Le Duc Tho package, Hummel now stated categorically that " . . . the [1973] Paris Agreement was so massively violated by Hanoi that we have no obligation to provide assistance, and in any case Congress has prohibited such assistance by law [under the Foreign Assistance Appropriation Act of 1976]."[7]

The U.S. embargo on trade and investment in Vietnam, in effect against North Vietnam since 1965, had been extended in May 1975 to all of Vietnam and Cambodia, and South Vietnamese assets in the United States were frozen.[8] The United States vetoed Hanoi's application for membership in the United Nations in 1975 and again in 1976, focusing on the missing-in-action question, which had surfaced as the most galling residue of the war. Shrill Vietnamese demands for reparations under the Paris Agreement contributed to congressional hostility.

Normalization of relations with Vietnam and putting the past behind us was a Carter campaign pledge, though it received little prominence in speeches and debates. The effort to normalize eventually foundered on three issues: Vietnam's demands for reparations, the Vietnamese invasion of Cambodia, and U.S. rapprochement with China. Together with the lingering uncertainty over the fate of American servicemen missing from the Vietnam War, these issues have continued to dog prospects for improved U.S.–Vietnam relations. They say much about contrasting American and Vietnamese perceptions of what the war was all about and reflect some of Indochina's enduring geopolitical facts of life. The bureaucratic antagonism between the State Department and the National Security Council (NSC) staff on a number of foreign policy issues, and the brittle relationship between Secretary of State Cyrus Vance and National Security Adviser Zbigniew Brzezinski, also complicated matters, particularly when normalization with China neared fruition in 1978.

President Carter seemed to look at an opening to Vietnam less as part of a new, comprehensive Asian strategy for the United States than as symbolically writing finis to an unhappy chapter in history.[9] In an October 1976 memorandum setting out specific goals and priorities for a Carter foreign policy, Cyrus

Vance placed heavy emphasis upon normalizing relations with Vietnam as "an opportunity for a new initiative . . . the Vietnamese are trying to find a balance between overdependence on either the Chinese or the Soviet Union. It is also to the interest of the U.S. that Vietnam not be so dependent."[10] Although Vance put normalization in the context of promoting the future development and stability of Southeast Asia, Vietnam was the dominant factor, and the 1976 memorandum made scant reference to the rest of the region. ASEAN, which had received declaratory importance beginning in 1977, began to take on more importance in American eyes only in 1978 after normalization showed signs of faltering and war in Cambodia loomed.

During the campaign, the Democrats had called for the "fullest possible accounting of MIAs." President Ford, on the other hand, to counter a charge of softness from the Republican right, had taken a tougher campaign line that retained the demand for a "full accounting" as a precondition to normalization. During 1976 U.S. and Vietnamese representatives held several official and private meetings on the missing-in-action issue. When President Carter took office, Vietnam was aware of American priorities, and the way had been paved for further contacts with the new administration. It is doubtful, however, that the Hanoi Politburo had by then really registered the depth of American feeling on this issue. Certainly they were ill-advised to use it as a bargaining chip ("bones for dollars" was the charge by U.S. critics of normalization) in the 1977–78 negotiations as had been done with the French after 1954.

President Carter's first foreign policy initiative was to send Leonard Woodcock, president of the United Auto Workers union, to Vietnam to test Hanoi's attitudes on normalization and determine specifically what the Vietnamese were prepared to do to meet U.S. requirements regarding MIAs. Secretary of State Cyrus Vance and his assistant secretary for East Asia and the Pacific, Richard Holbrooke, recognized that this was necessary in order to blunt domestic opposition to normalization from veterans groups and others outspokenly hostile to the victors in Hanoi. They believed the window of opportunity for such a move would not stay open long, and if the missing in action became a domestic political issue, normalization would be enormously complicated. Their judgment proved to be accurate.

Woodcock's delegation included Senator Mike Mansfield, Representative G.V. (Sonny) Montgomery, Ambassador Charles Yost, and human rights advocate Marian Wright Edelman. All except Montgomery had been critical in some measure of the American involvement in the war. Meeting with Prime Minister Pham Van Dong, Foreign Minister Nguyen Duy Trinh, and Deputy Foreign Minister Phan Hien (later Holbrooke's counterpart in the Paris normalization talks), Woodcock made a strong case for putting the missing-in-action issue to rest through the Vietnamese providing full information and as many remains as possible. Then, the two countries could move on to a new relationship that would dispel on both sides the war's pain and antagonisms.

The Vietnamese at first held fast to their demand for economic assistance under the terms of the February 1973 Nixon letter to Pham Van Dong pledging "best efforts to contribute to postwar reconstruction in North Vietnam without any political conditions . . . in the range of $3.25 billion in grant aid over five years."[11] Woodcock rejected this summarily by pointing out that the 1973 Paris Agreement, the basis for Nixon's pledge, had been destroyed by North Vietnam's massive violations in 1974–75. Eventually Phan Hien fell back to expressing a clear expectation of eventual humanitarian assistance in return for information on the missing in action. Woodcock deemed this response reasonable, as the demand for reparations under the defunct Paris Agreement appeared to have been dropped. Phan Hien announced the creation of a special office to seek information on the missing and to recover remains. He promised prompt action, making plain the Vietnamese position, however, that this humanitarian gesture merited an American response. As the delegation departed, the Vietnamese presented them with the remains of twelve U.S. servicemen as evidence of their sincerity, and Woodcock announced that the talks had "started a process which will improve the prospects for normalizing U.S.– Vietnamese relations."[12]

On one level the Woodcock mission was a remarkable success. It had broken the ice on the U.S.–Vietnam relationship, given hope of further progress on a sensitive American domestic concern, and apparently established a favorable atmosphere for formal negotiations toward diplomatic relations. Yet there was also an element of imprecision and false hope. The seeds of miscalculation on both sides, which bedeviled subsequent negotiations, may have been planted in this initial encounter and by the almost euphoric reaction in Washington, including statements by the president himself.

The relationship between "humanitarian aid" and "full accounting" for MIAs was left vague as to timing and definition. Although Woodcock had tried to separate the issues, the Vietnamese clung to the notion of an inevitable quid pro quo quality to normalization. In Phan Hien's words after Woodcock had adamantly rejected linkage, "they are separate issues but closely interrelated."[13] The Vietnamese continued to operate on the presumption that the United States owed Vietnam economic assistance legally and morally, that American public opinion would pressure the administration to pay this debt of conscience, and that humanitarian aid could cover a wide spectrum of things their shattered country needed. Woodcock's response may have encouraged this idea, as did President Carter's statement after the delegation's return that "if, in normalization of relations, there evolves trade, normal aid processes, then I would respond well."[14] The president left open at what point aid might come— as part of a normalization deal or after normalization had taken place. Whatever the definition, the Vietnamese chose to believe that the United States had not in fact foreclosed the possibility of large-scale official aid.

Second, there was no clear understanding on what Vietnam would do in the future to resolve the MIA problem. No plan of action was drawn up; the matter was left in the realm of imprecise Vietnamese good intentions and unclear American expectations. President Carter's remarks following the commission's return acted as a signal to the Vietnamese: "I think this is about all they can do . . . I don't have any way [to] prove that they have accounted for all those about whom they have information. . . . But I think so far as I can discern, they have acted in good faith."[15] The report of Representative Montgomery's House Select Committee on Missing Persons in Southeast Asia several months before had rejected the possibility of live Americans being held captive in Indochina, and it had stated flatly that "a total accounting by the Indochinese governments is not possible and should not be expected."[16] The Woodcock Commission report had reiterated this. Thus the Vietnamese had reason to believe that MIAs, while not crossed off the American negotiating agenda, had receded in priority and could be handled satisfactorily with an unspecified minimum effort on Hanoi's part.

Moreover, at this stage the Vietnamese mind-set was, in Lenin's words, "dizzy from success." Having conquered the South and humbled a superpower, while suffering immense human and material losses in the process, the Vietnamese leaders seemed blind to a central reality: Hanoi needed normalization far more than Washington. The United States was not the demandeur despite its almost plaintive insistence on MIA cooperation. Having witnessed the power of the antiwar movement in behalf of their cause, the Vietnamese apparently believed that similar public pressure would force the Carter administration's hand. Friends from the antiwar movement encouraged the Vietnamese to believe that the American guilt complex would yield multibillion dollar reparations as part of normalization.

Despite indications of flexibility, the Vietnamese remained adamant on aid. This attitude turned out to be an extraordinary blunder that cost valuable months during the 1977–78 negotiations before reality finally dawned.

It was a year of frustration. U.S. and Vietnamese negotiators met in Paris in May, June, and December 1977. The United States had already pledged to support Vietnam's membership in the United Nations (UN). During the first meeting in May,

Holbrooke proposed unconditional establishment of relations, after which the U.S. trade embargo would be lifted. Phan Hien, however, again placed economic assistance front and center as a precondition to normalization, linking it to cooperation on the missing in action. Worse, he restated Vietnam's demands at a press conference after the meeting, producing immediate congressional reaction in the form of an amendment to the House of Representatives' State Department authorization bill prohibiting use of any funds "for the purpose of negotiating reparations, aid or any other form of payment."[17] Later, the Senate followed suit with an amendment requiring U.S. opposition to loans to Vietnam by international financial institutions.[18]

Then, just prior to the June meeting, the Vietnamese published the text of the 1973 Nixon letter and rekindled their public campaign in the United States for aid. This was another tactical blunder. As Nayan Chanda points out, "those who marched on the Pentagon calling for peace were not there now to demand help for Vietnam."[19] Hanoi's demands only served to arouse conservative criticism of the normalization gambit, and congressional actions narrowed still further Holbrooke's room for maneuver—the possibility of even humanitarian aid after normalization became remote. The window for normalization had begun to close earlier than expected.

The June meeting produced information on 20 MIAs and from Phan Hien private expressions of flexibility as to the form and amount of U.S. assistance the Vietnamese expected. "Contributions to heal the wounds of war" became the standard term of reference—but Hanoi did not publicly renounce its demand for reparations, a crucial factor to resuscitating the negotiations.

Further movement was blocked when the State Department learned that the Vietnamese permanent representative to the UN, Ambassador Dinh Ba Thi, had received stolen classified documents from a United States Information Agency (USIA) officer who, through his amateur espionage, hoped to gain the release of his girlfriend from Vietnam. Although the extent of damage to U.S. security interests could not be immediately ascertained, the June and December 1977 negotiations became especially delicate from the American perspective.*

When the USIA officer, Ronald Humphrey, and his associate, David Truong, were arrested in January 1978, and Ambassador Thi declared *persona non grata,* any hope for a fourth Paris round in February or March was dashed.[20] No negotiations were feasible during the well-publicized Humphrey-Truong trial, which lasted until June 1978. This small-time spying escapade was a gratuitous blunder by Thi that cost Vietnam dearly on a vastly more important front.†

During the winter of 1977–78 intelligence became available on the brutal incursions into southern Vietnamese border provinces by the Chinese-backed Khmer Rouge regime of Pol Pot. By early summer 1978, ominous evidence surfaced that indicated that Vietnam, stung by thousands of casualties (mostly civilians) on its own territory, was preparing to invade Cambodia with the intent of deposing Pol Pot.[21] Given Thailand's vulnerability on its eastern border and presumed Vietnamese expansionist impulses, such an action raised alarming security implications for the region. Wags in Bangkok predicted that the city's massive traffic jams would stop even Vietnamese tanks. In 1978, however, just three years after the American debacle, few officials in Bangkok and Washington doubted the Vietnamese ability to sweep across Thailand's Korat plateau in a matter of days after conquering Cambodia, though such an inflammatory action seemed unlikely even for the headstrong Vietnamese.

---

* In October, negotiations were also impeded by Hanoi's handling of the *Brillig,* an American pleasure yacht apprehended in Vietnamese coastal waters whose crew were accused of drug-running and imprisoned in Saigon. Washington urged Hanoi to resolve the matter quickly, but weeks went by without the International Red Cross being allowed access. The incident stirred interest by the media and rumblings from Congress. Hanoi finally released the *Brillig*'s crew after payment of a sizable fine, but the next Paris meeting had been further delayed.

† The Vietnamese reaction to the Humphrey-Truong trial was remarkably subdued. It is not known if Ambassador Thi's activities were authorized by Hanoi, but not long after his return from New York, Hanoi Radio reported that Thi had been "killed in a road accident."

At least as important was the quickening pace of Washington's normalization negotiations with the People's Republic of China. National Security Adviser Zbigniew Brzezinski and his Asia deputy, Michel Oksenberg, held that normalization with Vietnam had become incompatible with normalization with China, a process moving toward fruition but still in the balance. In their eyes, the China gambit was far more valuable than a relationship with Vietnam. Early in the Carter administration Vance and Holbrooke expressed the view that a relationship with Hanoi would benefit long-term U.S. strategic interests, including the U.S.–Soviet and U.S.–China strategic equations. Brzezinski (who was fixated on the China connection as a way to constrain and harass the Soviets) believed that normalizing with Vietnam, China's ancient enemy that was about to attack China's Cambodian ally, would damage and perhaps derail establishment of full diplomatic relations with China (there had been liaison offices in the respective capitals since 1973). He was ultimately joined in this view by Leonard Woodcock, who had become U.S. Liaison Office chief in Beijing.[22]

During this period the administration's concerns over growing Soviet-Vietnamese ties were confirmed. For two years after 1975, Vietnam, wary of China's reaction, had resisted Soviet pressure to join the Council for Mutual Economic Assistance (COMECON). In late June 1978, however, the Vietnamese signed up, thereby putting their economy on the road to greater reliance on trade with and economic assistance from the Soviet bloc. This may have reflected disappointment over the course of normalization talks with the United States, but it also reflected Hanoi's recognition that only the Soviet Union could provide quick help to a Vietnamese economy that had gone from bad to worse since 1975, thanks to coerced collectivization and harsh repression of South Vietnam's free market practices. The decision to join COMECON was another nail in normalization's coffin. Long term, it would make economic and political relations with the West far more difficult.

A few days after the end of the Humphrey-Truong trial (both were found guilty and sentenced to jail), with normalization prospects dim, the Vietnamese accepted a long-standing U.S. invitation to visit the Joint Casualty Resolution Center and Central Identification Laboratory in Hawaii, the site of technical efforts to identify MIA remains. The ostensible purpose was to signal their readiness to cooperate more actively in resolving the MIA issue. During the four-day "technical" meeting in Honolulu, however, Vu Hoang, a senior Foreign Ministry official and the delegation chief, made clear in private that Vietnam had dropped its aid precondition and wanted normalization on American terms "by Labor Day or at the latest Thanksgiving." No mention was made of Christmas, the day on which Vietnam invaded Cambodia. Vu Hoang suggested that giant C-5A aircraft be used to bring in materials to build a U.S. embassy in Hanoi "with a big commercial section." U.S. Navy Seabees would be welcome to oversee the construction.[23] Although Vu Hoang's statement seemed explicit and unequivocal, it was nonetheless a trial balloon hoisted at the working level and required high-level expression. The message was conveyed immediately to the State Department, where it became enmeshed in the bureaucratic infighting with the National Security Council staff. A Vietnamese proposal shortly thereafter for another Paris meeting in August 1978 was not accepted by the United States.

The Vietnamese did give public hints of flexibility during the summer, notably Phan Hien's July 10 statement in Tokyo that "a new forward-looking attitude is being shown by the Vietnamese side." Phan Hien said Vietnam would not seek aid as a precondition for normalization but, when pressed to clarify, added "if they [the Americans] come with something in their hands, they will be more welcomed than if they come with empty hands."[24] Congressional delegations visiting Hanoi received some MIA remains but could not pry a convincing renunciation of the aid demand from the top leadership.

Thus the impression that Hanoi was still playing fast and loose on preconditions severely handicapped the State Department in its battle with the NSC staff over the compatibility of the twin-track normalization efforts with Beijing and Hanoi. Only on September 27, 1978, in New York, was Holbrooke (with

Oksenberg present) finally able to extract from Foreign Minister Nguyen Co Thach the absolute acceptance of normalization of relations without preconditions that Holbrooke had sought for eighteen months. Acceptance, however, was *ad referendum* to Washington, and at this point only President Carter could resolve the conflict between the competing U.S. strategies toward China and Southeast Asia. On October 11, the president accepted the Brzezinski-Woodcock recommendation and decided to defer normalization with Vietnam. The reasons, given retrospectively, were concern over the implications of growing Vietnamese hostility toward Cambodia, expanding Soviet-Vietnamese ties, and the tide of "boat people"—refugees fleeing repression in Vietnam. The "China card," however, was decisive.

On November 2, 1978, Vietnam and the Soviet Union signed a mutual security treaty. U.S.–Vietnam normalization collapsed before the year was out. With the December 1978 Vietnamese invasion of Cambodia and the overthrow of Pol Pot's regime in January 1979, followed in February by China's three-week punitive expedition into northern Vietnam, the geopolitical chessboard was frozen. The Soviets installed a military presence at Cam Ranh Bay and Danang, and the United States and China, which had consummated their normalization in December 1978, embarked on a multifaceted relationship that would have direct strategic impact upon both the Soviet Union and Vietnam.

Timing, of course, is all. In 1977 the time was ripe for Vietnam and the United States to get together. A sympathetic new American administration was in office with some latitude in foreign affairs; feeling about MIAs was strong but had not coalesced; and there was adequate support on Capitol Hill for normalization. Vietnam was pro-Soviet but had not taken the plunge into COMECON or signed a security pact; there was genuine debate in the Vietnamese Politburo on future multiple links with the capitalist world versus near-total reliance on the socialist bloc. China was aware of how normalization of U.S.–Vietnam relations might help blunt Vietnam's growing dependence on the Soviets. ASEAN was not opposed to normalization if it would help tame the Vietnamese tiger, and indeed its members warily pursued the same track.

Why did normalization, something both sides genuinely sought, fail? Several reasons stand out. Vietnam's flat demand for economic assistance as a precondition, no matter how justified in the eyes of the Politburo, prevented consummation during the first six months of the Carter administration when the window was wide open. This failure to perceive objective reality, that prized Marxist precept for political action, was the key strategic blunder of the entire period.* After Hanoi's 1975 military conquest, reparations by any other name were never in the cards. The Humphrey-Truong affair delayed negotiations at a crucial moment, when the window was still half open.

The prevarications and coy zigzagging as Hanoi gradually modified, or appeared to modify, its position wasted valuable time. When Thach finally conceded, other factors in Asia (in particular normalization of relations with China) had become dominant for the United States. Elsewhere, the Carter administration's foreign policy troubles were beginning to pile up: the fight over the Panama Canal treaty, rumblings in Iran, the SALT II negotiations, Angola. It was no time for a questionable venture with a former—and victorious—foe.

Normalization—what if it had taken place? Historians will debate the wisdom of each side's judgment on the strategy and tactics of this aborted 1977–78 effort. Clearly, Vietnam missed an opportunity. Hanoi could have had normalization by mid-1977 on better terms (including good prospects for humanitarian aid later on) than it agreed to in late 1978.

Some analysts claim with no less certainty that the United States missed a valuable opportunity in mid-1978. Even granting Hanoi's blunders, prevarications, and ultimate intentions, it is arguable that the Carter administration in general, and the National Security Council staff in particular, approached the question of Vietnam in a narrow manner that gave unwar-

---

* An earlier grand misperception was the Politburo's judgment that the South Vietnamese populace would rise up and join the Viet Cong during the 1968 Tet offensive.

ranted weight to Deng Xiaoping's hostility toward Vietnam and in the end shortchanged U.S. strategic interests in the region.

Normalization early in 1977, after the first Paris meeting, might have helped nudge Vietnam in the direction of moderation in internal reforms and economic relations with the West and away from COMECON. The Soviet bear hug might have been avoided, delayed, or softened. China would have had less cause for anger over Vietnamese "ingratitude." Vietnam might have been more inclined to mobilize international opinion against Pol Pot early in 1978 and perhaps head off the bloody Khmer Rouge incursions that precipitated the December invasion. In brief, Vietnam would have had more options domestically and diplomatically, and the future might have been somewhat different.

It is unlikely that normalization after mid-1978 would have had any such effect. By then, Vietnam had decided that the Khmer Rouge were intolerable and that military action to remove them from power was the only cure. By the summer Hanoi was moving quickly to organize a Cambodian liberation front, the precursor of the People's Republic of Kampuchea (PRK) under Heng Samrin and Hun Sen, high-ranking Khmer Rouge commanders who had defected from Pol Pot and taken refuge in Vietnam. China, which earlier had sent Madame Deng Yingchao, the widow of Zhou Enlai, to Phnom Penh in an effort to moderate the Khmer Rouge excesses against Vietnam, had given up trying to restrain the Khmer Rouge.[25] Instead, China decided to back its murderous ally to the hilt against Soviet-sponsored Vietnamese "regional hegemonism." This served, in turn, to harden Vietnam's position and drive it further toward the Soviets, who warmly reciprocated by supplying additional arms. Thus, by the time Thach relinquished Vietnamese preconditions to normalization in September 1978, the leading players in this Greek drama had embarked on conflicting, probably unalterable, courses. Moreover, it is difficult to avoid the conclusion that Thach's purpose at that late date was mainly to blunt American reaction to an inevitable invasion of Cambodia. With U.S.–China normalization in the wind, this was goal enough.

What if there had been no invasion of Cambodia? It is arguable that if Vietnam had normalized with the United States in 1977, with all the benefits that would have accrued, the invasion of 1978 would still have been undertaken, but perhaps with one major difference. Vietnam might have chosen to stop at Phnom Penh, rather than go all the way to the Thai border. Having performed the good deed of deposing Pol Pot, it could have called for international assistance and declared its readiness to quit Cambodia under certain conditions. Vietnam might have emerged as something of a hero instead of the villain, and the anti-Vietnamese resistance might never have been organized. Finally, ASEAN and China might not have considered it necessary to regenerate the political and military strength of the Khmer Rouge.

This scenario is highly speculative, of course. It is equally arguable that, with an American connection in their pocket, the Vietnamese would have been even more emboldened. Once they had invaded, it seems probable that they would have settled for nothing short of a Cambodian regime responsive to Hanoi's influence, if not control. This would have represented the same unacceptable situation for China, namely "Vietnamese regional hegemonism," as obtains today.

On the other side of the coin, it is hard to imagine how the Khmer exiles would have been able to organize themselves without the decade of stalemate that followed 1978. In 1989, at least, it is possible that Sihanouk and company may eventually participate in some sort of coalition government with the Vietnamese-backed regime in Phnom Penh; in 1979, the chances would have been very small.

If Vietnam had not removed Pol Pot, who would have done the job? This is an extremely painful question, because in 1978 few people in the West, including the United States, paid much attention to the reports of the Khmer Rouge's mass atrocities, despite several well-documented and shocking exposés of the brutal policies that were published in 1977 and 1978.[26] The American embassy in Bangkok, the State Department, and some intelligence community officials were aware through reports from refugees of what transpired after April 1975. But the full horror of the Khmer Rouge's genocide (the Tuol Sleng torture center in Phnom Penh and the Choeung Ek killing fields nearby are best known but only a tiny sample of the total) was given publicity only when Vietnam occupied Cambodia. Neither Thailand, nor ASEAN, nor certainly the United States would have been prepared to intervene in Democratic Kampuchea's (DK) internal affairs to stop the horror.

Perhaps Vietnam would not have retaliated militarily in 1978 had it not been hurt so badly by the Khmer Rouge attacks in the delta. Yet one need not condone Vietnam's aggression, which was performed for reasons of national security—as defined by Hanoi—and its regional ambition, to admit that Pol Pot and his murderous band of "social reformers" would probably still be in power today were it not for the Vietnamese actions.[27]

Again, this conjecture is of more than philosophical interest. In 1989 and 1990, as the United States considers policy options regarding the future governance of Cambodia, it will have to choose the least worst of several unpalatable courses.

Bilaterally, when normalization diplomacy ceased in 1978, Vietnam also ceased any semblance of cooperation on MIAs. Normalization was dead in the water. On May 30, 1979, State Department Deputy Assistant Secretary Robert Oakley warned Vietnam Ambassador to the United Nations Ha Van Lau that Hanoi should "act with restraint in Southeast Asia, especially regarding Thailand" and made plain U.S. concern "about the long-term implications of the growing Soviet military presence in Vietnam." Subsequently the United States publicly rejected normalization as long as Vietnam occupied Cambodia and threatened its neighbors.[28]

Only in the early years of the Reagan administration did talks on humanitarian concerns resume. MIA discussions again became the main vehicle of communication with Vietnam. Three more issues were added to the dialogue: emigration of Vietnamese children of American fathers (the "Amerasian children" program), the Orderly Departure Program (ODP) permitting emigration of Vietnamese with connections to the United States, and the U.S. attempt to gain the exit from Vietnam of former inmates of Vietnamese "reeducation camps."

In February 1982 Deputy Assistant Secretary of Defense for International Security Affairs Richard Armitage visited Hanoi to probe possibilities of renewing Vietnamese POW/MIA cooperation. The next two years saw expansion of technical level meetings, and in 1985 Vietnam permitted excavation of a B-52 crash site near Hanoi by U.S. teams. About one hundred MIA remains were repatriated as a result of this fresh effort. Hanoi announced in 1985 that it would make a unilateral effort to resolve the MIA issue within two years. To test the water, in early 1986, Armitage (by then promoted to assistant secretary of defense) and Assistant Secretary of State for East Asian and Pacific Affairs Paul Wolfowitz led the highest-level American executive branch delegation to Vietnam since the 1977 Woodcock mission. They received more assurances of unconditional cooperation on POW/MIAs and some indications of greater flexibility on other issues.

On humanitarian matters—and on broader policy issues to the limited extent they were addressed at all—the Reagan administration's view of Indochina was shaped day-to-day by concern over the POW/MIA issue. Lurid publicity, stimulated in part through the "Rambo" movies, was given to rumors that American servicemen were still being held prisoner in Vietnam or elsewhere in Indochina, and reports of "live sightings" of prisoners caused greater concern. The administration was roundly criticized by activist veteran groups for not doing more to rescue the supposed prisoners, and several private soldier-of-fortune forays into Laos were launched from Thai soil.

Vietnam found the humanitarian dialogue useful during this period; it was the only means to entice the United States into a more active role in Indochinese affairs. Hanoi saw it as a tool to keep ASEAN, which worried that U.S. preoccupation with POW/MIAs might undermine the Cambodia strategy, on edge regarding American intentions. On a broader level, Hanoi's longer-term strategy was to play U.S. influence off against China and the Soviet Union, and to seek U.S. help to revive the Vietnamese economy after normalization. Humanitarian dialogue thus became the music for the U.S.–Vietnam mating dance.

Cambodia was the limiting factor, since it made no sense from the Politburo's perspective to grant the Americans concessions on humanitarian matters at a time when Cambodia was frozen and normalization of relations therefore out of the question. Improvement of the bilateral climate, however, was valuable to the Vietnamese, and they listened attentively as every congressional or executive branch visitor to Hanoi reiterated the same theme: although humanitarian affairs were separate from politics (Cambodia), normalization would proceed more smoothly if there were sustained progress on those issues beforehand. It is fair to say that Hanoi came to understand this subtle nonlinkage and saw the political value of doing the honorable thing on these questions—at the proper time. It is not surprising that the pace of the U.S.–Vietnam humanitarian dialogue picked up after 1986 as the Cambodia stalemate began to break.

4

THE REGIONAL FOCUS

On Christmas Day 1978 Vietnam invaded Cambodia. Striking from bases along the border, Vietnamese tanks rolled quickly along the main highways of eastern Cambodia toward the Mekong River in a coordinated, multipronged attack. Within a few days the Vietnamese captured the provincial capital Kratie (where, ironically, only a decade before they had trained and equipped Khmer Rouge forces to fight the Lon Nol government) and reached the banks of the Mekong at Kompong Cham and Neak Luong. With surprising ease, the Vietnamese routed the Khmer Rouge defenders, entered Phnom Penh on January 7, 1979, and within a few days swept west to the Thai border.

With the removal of the Pol Pot government and installation of a pro-Vietnam regime in Phnom Penh, a new era in the Indochina drama began. The history of the decade of the 1980s has centered on the struggle between Vietnam, its Cambodian surrogate, and the Soviet Union, on one side, and ASEAN, China, the anti-Vietnamese Cambodian resistance movements, and the United States, on the other.

The issue has been "irreversibility"—whether Vietnam's occupation of Cambodia would continue indefinitely. ASEAN and its international supporters have refused to accept this *fait accompli*. The effort has been to rebuff what China calls "Vietnamese regional hegemonism" and what ASEAN and the United States consider aggression by Vietnam against a neighbor, albeit one with a despicable government.

The vehicle for Vietnam's "liberation" of Cambodia was the Kampuchean National United Front for National Salvation (KNUFNS), a composite group comprising ethnic Cambodians living in South Vietnam, disaffected Khmer Rouge and other native Cambodians who had fled across the border to escape Pol Pot's rule, and Vietnamese who had previously lived in Cambodia. KNUFNS had been organized, trained, and equipped by Vietnam for precisely this contingency, which took on some urgency as Khmer Rouge attacks increased in 1978. It was KNUFNS that rode into Phnom Penh on Vietnamese tanks in January 1979.

The 1978 invasion of Cambodia marked the beginning of a second phase in U.S. policy toward Indochina following the Vietnam War. This phase was characterized by a heightened U.S. appreciation of the importance of regional cooperation among the noncommunist Southeast Asian countries, by a certain deference to ASEAN, and by the Carter administration's effort to dispel the notion that East Asia and the Pacific had dropped out of sight on Washington's list of global priorities because of Vietnam. "The United States is, and will remain, an Asian and Pacific power" was intoned in major policy speeches during this period in order to reassure our friends that the United States had no intention of abandoning the strategic field to either China or the Soviet Union.[1] Though this was "credibility" by another name, the emphasis was upon East Asia for its own sake, not just as a symbol of U.S. reliability everywhere else in the world, and it was Washington's Asian leitmotiv for the four Carter years.

With the eclipse of Vietnam normalization in 1978, successive U.S. administrations dealt with Indochina affairs (except for MIAs) through the filter of relations with ASEAN. Cambodia was the region's prime political irritant, but in Washington's view it was a problem for which ASEAN, not the United States, should assume prime responsibility. Reviewing his tenure as secretary of state, Cyrus Vance writes: "The Carter administration had reversed the previous policy of ignoring ASEAN and dealing with its members only on a bilateral state-to-state basis." Vice President Mondale made a trip to Southeast Asia in May 1978 to celebrate ASEAN as a rising star in the U.S. foreign policy firmament, and Secretary Vance chaired the first significant discussions in August 1978 in Washington with fourteen ministers from ASEAN countries.[2]

Founded as an economic and social coordinating body, ASEAN's most significant accomplishments have not been in economic cooperation but in political affairs as the international leader in rebuffing Vietnamese aggression in Cambodia. ASEAN's organizers understood clearly the diverse interests and uneven levels of development of the member countries, whose industries and commodities were for the most part competitive with one another rather than complementary. Decision making was based upon the Malay *musjawarah* principle of careful consensus building. Each member could retain or form whatever defense arrangements with other countries, in or outside ASEAN, it deemed necessary for national security.

While security concerns were the catalyst of ASEAN's consolidation, the Association nonetheless eschewed the connotation of a regional security arrangement. Its Zone of Peace, Freedom, and Neutrality (ZOPFAN) reflected hopes and fears found to some degree in all the ASEAN countries, an idealistic goal that few expect to be realized soon. Similarly the Southeast Asia Nuclear Weapons–Free Zone (SEANWFZ) reflected a general nervousness in the Pacific about nuclear testing, the environment, and unwanted spin-off from great power rivalries.

The annual ASEAN ministerial conferences have (with the exception of 1982) been attended by the U.S. secretary of state, most recently in July 1989 by James Baker in Brunei. While economic and trade relations have often dominated the agenda over the past eleven years, both ASEAN and the United States have come to realize they have much to talk about in the political sphere, as coequals rather than as patron-clients. Beyond trade, the massive outflow of Indochinese refugees and the issue of Cambodia have been two perennial issues.

In 1978–79 a tidal wave of Vietnamese refugees took to the sea to escape the Hanoi government's draconian economic and social policies in South Vietnam. Boat arrivals on the shores of Thailand, Malaysia, Singapore, and Indonesia began to overwhelm those countries' resources, reaching the level of 75,000 refugees per month by early 1979. Hanoi's policy of callous expulsion added weight to the arguments in Washington against normalization of relations in the summer of 1978.

With the Vietnamese invasion of Cambodia in December and the collapse of the Pol Pot regime, hundreds of thousands of Khmers fled across the border to seek refuge in Thailand from the fighting, imposing an immense burden on the eastern third of that country. In the north, Lao and Hmong refugees continued their flight across the Mekong River begun in the summer of 1975 and spurred subsequently by Pathet Lao repression, thus adding to Thailand's problems.

The United States became the leader of an international rescue, relief, and resettlement effort. At the time of the June 1979 Tokyo Summit, in the parallel bilateral "summit" with Japan, President Carter authorized doubling the U.S. Indochina refugee intake to 17,000 per month, an annual total of 168,000.* In July Vice President Mondale led the U.S. delegation to a conference on refugees in Geneva that opened up resettlement doors in other countries. According to Cyrus Vance, Mondale's speech in Geneva was the turning point in the international assistance effort: "The policy he outlined that day will long stand as one of the most significant acts of the Carter administration."[3] Ten years later, at another United Nations–sponsored international conference on Indochina refugees (again held in Geneva, in June 13–14, 1989) the climate of opinion had changed markedly, as described in Chapter 9.

The situation in Cambodia, however, was at the heart of both the U.S. relationship with ASEAN and its policy toward Vietnam after 1979. In order to force Vietnam to modify its position on Cambodia, ASEAN wielded both carrots and sticks. As carrots, ASEAN offered to negotiate a peaceful settlement in Cambodia and a bright promise of economic and commercial relations. At the March 1980 meeting between Indonesian President Suharto and Malaysian Prime Minister Tun Hussein, at Kuantan, Malaysia, Vietnam's security concerns with regard to Cambodia had been recognized, and the two leaders disassociated their countries from China's announced policy of "bleeding

---

* Limited by its immigration policy, Japan agreed as a quid pro quo to fund 50 percent of the Indochina budget of the Office of the United Nations High Commissioner for Refugees (UNHCR).

Vietnam white." Although this was not a formal ASEAN position, not long thereafter at the July 1981 UN International Conference on Kampuchea (ICK), ASEAN called for a peace settlement in Cambodia that would not "pose a threat to or be used against the security, sovereignty and territorial integrity of other states, especially those sharing a common border with Kampuchea." While continuing to condemn Vietnam's actions on this and other occasions in the early years of the occupation, ASEAN sought to convince Vietnam of the wisdom of a negotiated political settlement in return for a cooperative, economically attractive relationship with noncommunist Southeast Asia. In these early years, Hanoi was not prepared to modify its position.

ASEAN's sticks were diplomatic and economic isolation of Hanoi and the PRK, the creation of the Coalition Government of Democratic Kampuchea (CGDK), and retention of Cambodia's seat in the United Nations for Democratic Kampuchea. The U.S. embargo on trade and investment, in place since earlier war days, was an essential element in maintaining the ASEAN pressure. Japan, the European Community (EC), and other potential aid donors or investors were reluctant to break ranks as long as the United States held fast. The denial of American maritime oil technology to Vietnam through third countries and prevention of major development loans from international financial institutions were critical.

The CGDK was formed in June 1982 by ASEAN and China, with American blessings, as a tripartite coalition of Pol Pot's DK, Prince Norodom Sihanouk's National United Front for an Independent, Peaceful, Neutral, and Cooperative Cambodia (FUNCINPEC, the acronym in French), and the Khmer People's National Liberation Front (KPNLF) under a former Cambodian prime minister, Son Sann. Sihanouk was president, Son Sann prime minister, and Khmer Rouge leader Khieu Samphan vice president and foreign minister. Sihanouk and Son Sann have pursued a loose, sometimes acrimonious alliance; together they constitute the noncommunist resistance (NCR), as distinguished from the Khmer Rouge.

41

Both components of the NCR detest the Khmer Rouge, who were responsible for the deaths of approximately two million Cambodians between 1975 and 1978. Many were the families and associates of the people who make up the Khmer Rouge's CGDK allies today. (Sihanouk claims he lost 40 relatives.) The CGDK has one common bond: hatred for the Vietnamese and a determination to remove them from Cambodia.

China's big stick was the Khmer Rouge, the most powerful military arm of the CGDK's insurgency. The essential ingredient in China's support for the Khmer Rouge was (and remains) the cooperation of Thailand, through whose ports China funneled supplies. The foundation for de facto Sino-Thai alliance to resist the Vietnamese occupation of Cambodia through reviving and strengthening the defeated Khmer Rouge was laid in the first weeks of 1979, well before the formation of the CGDK.[4] Another stick was the long border between China and Vietnam. To emphasize its displeasure over Hanoi's actions in Cambodia, China invaded Vietnam's northern provinces in February 1979. Although the invasion cost the Chinese heavy casualties and was eventually contained by Vietnam's tenacious counterattacks, it wreaked havoc on already destitute areas of North Vietnam. It also had the effect in the following years of forcing Vietnam to station some of its best military units on the northern border in anticipation of a second "lesson."

In September 1979, the United States supported the ASEAN and Chinese demand that Democratic Kampuchea retain its credentials in the United Nations. It also backed the creation of the Khmer resistance using the remnants of Pol Pot's forces as the nucleus. These decisions were viewed by the Carter administration as vital to supporting ASEAN's rejection of irreversibility. National Security Affairs Adviser Brzezinski was convinced that Cambodia was a "proxy" war between the Soviet Union and China, and this alone justified supporting the anti-Vietnamese forces regardless of their character. In Washington, preventing a single power from establishing hegemony over Southeast Asia remained a basic objective; Vietnam's continued occupation of Cambodia supported the assumption that an

"Indochina Federation" was Hanoi's goal. Memories of the collapse in 1975 of the Lon Nol and Thieu regimes in Cambodia and South Vietnam were still fresh.

At the same time, the atrocious conduct of the Khmer Rouge while in power, the full dimensions of which had become evident after the removal of Pol Pot, presented a painful dilemma for the administration. Describing the credentials vote in the UN General Assembly in September 1979, Cyrus Vance states, "I had weighed the pros and cons of this issue for weeks. Days before the final vote, I had come to the conclusion that, unpleasant as it was to contemplate voting, even implicitly, for the Khmer Rouge, we could not afford the far-reaching consequences of a vote that would isolate us from ASEAN, Japan, China, our ANZUS treaty partners, and most of our European allies, and put us in a *losing* [Vance's emphasis] minority with Moscow, Hanoi, and Havana."[5] In Vance's view, a vote not to seat the DK, by appearing to legitimize a forcible takeover of one country by another, would have gained the United States nothing and cost it much.

For Brzezinski, the objective was to enhance the U.S.–China strategic relationship in the common anti-Soviet effort. Elizabeth Becker, veteran reporter and analyst of Cambodian affairs, writes that Brzezinski claimed credit for persuading Thailand to cooperate with China to rebuild the Khmer Rouge on the occasion of his visit to Thailand in the spring of 1979. She quotes Brzezinski: "I encouraged the Chinese to support Pol Pot. I encouraged the Thai to help the DK. The question was how to help the Cambodian people. Pol Pot was an abomination. We could never support him but China could."[6] In his own memoirs Brzezinski is silent on his precise role in building up the Khmer Rouge. But in describing preparations for his May 1979 visit to Beijing he notes that the president empowered him to engage the Chinese "in a broad political-strategic review of the global situation" and to express U.S. determination to respond assertively to "Soviet proxy expansionism around the world." One of his objectives, Brzezinski states, was to persuade China "to facilitate the emergence of an independent Cambodian government that enjoys the support of its people."[7]

Each year at the United Nations, ASEAN rounded up virtually unanimous Western and Third World support for keeping Cambodia's seat in the hands of Democratic Kampuchea, thus isolating the PRK diplomatically by preventing recognition outside the Soviet bloc, with the exception of India. This isolation was essential to the strategy of forcing Vietnam to negotiate a political solution. At the same time, the United States was frequently perceived as supporting the Chinese rather than the ASEAN view of the Khmer Rouge role. The most egregious example was at the July 1981 International Conference on Kampuchea when ASEAN, in the drafting of the final resolution, was obliged to drop its call for disarming the Khmer factions and for holding free elections under an interim administration in a future Cambodia settlement.[8] China successfully fought off even implied criticism of the Khmer Rouge in the resolution. Beijing was supported by the United States against ASEAN in this effort. The U.S. tendency to view Cambodia policy mainly in the context of its potential impact upon relations with China persisted through the Reagan administration. The implications were not lost upon ASEAN, and the memory lingers to this day among some of our best friends in Southeast Asia.

In analyzing the U.S. decisions, it is perhaps not difficult to arrive at the same conclusion as Secretary Vance that, no matter how morally offensive it was to vote for the DK, no other reasonable choice in 1979 presented itself. The more difficult question, however, is whether the United States failed in succeeding years, particularly after the formation of the CGDK in 1982, to do all it could to disassociate itself from the distasteful reality of the Khmer Rouge presence in the CGDK and to examine soberly the longer-term implications.

U.S. financial and nonlethal material contributions to the noncommunist resistance factions of the CGDK were small during this period but politically significant. While precise figures are not publicly available, covert assistance on the order of $10 to $15 million annually has reportedly been provided to these groups since 1984, or earlier.[9] The level of Chinese aid to the Khmer Rouge has been many times higher than the combined U.S. and ASEAN figure for the noncommunist groups and has included quantities of lethal assistance. In 1985, to the administration's discomfort, Congress under the leadership of Representative Stephen Solarz (D-N.Y.), chairman of the House Foreign Affairs Committee's Subcommittee on Asia and the Pacific, authorized up to $5 million in overt aid for education, training, and logistical support for resistance groups operating out of Thailand; this program was funded at about $3.5 million annually. As noted in subsequent chapters, Solarz' aid initiative has taken on substantial significance in the end game negotiations toward a Cambodia settlement.

Looking back at the confusion and American sense of defeat in the years immediately after 1975, it is worth noting that the U.S.–ASEAN relationship is a relatively recent geopolitical phenomenon which, now, we take for granted. With two countries of the ASEAN group—Thailand and the Philippines—the United States had a history of generally warm bilateral relations, enhanced by security treaties. With the others, which were emerging from colonial status, the bilateral relationships were still in the formative stage. The creation of ASEAN in 1967 and its evolution after 1975 provided an important new dimension to the U.S. ability to relate to noncommunist Southeast Asia as a region, and for the most part this has been advantageous to American interests. There have been few dramatic events to mark this phenomenon but rather a steady growth in the ASEAN countries' ability, individually and collectively, to look after their own backyard. "Regional resilience," the Indonesian term of art for noncommunist Southeast Asia's dynamism and spirit of self-confidence, represents one of the most significant, if little noted, developments in Asia since World War II.

None of this is immutable, however, and as the ASEAN countries have matured, so have their interests and relationships with one another begun to shift and evolve. Economic competition is increasingly apparent. Thailand has launched a new vision of its role in the region as at the heart of concentric geopolitical rings: an inner ring (the "golden land") of itself, Burma, and Indochina; a middle ring of the other ASEAN states; and an outer ring of the greater Asia and Pacific region. Thailand thus becomes, in its own view, the development window on the world for Vietnam, Laos, and Cambodia as they carry out their reconstruction and, it is hoped, emerge from their socialist fetters. On the other fronts, ASEAN and the United States also have a variety of trade differences which must be addressed bilaterally as well as collectively.

ASEAN is experiencing greater difficulty in maintaining a united position now that it is in the midst of earnest negotiations toward a Cambodia settlement. This has made more urgent the recasting of U.S. policy from "let ASEAN take the lead" into more sophisticated—and more independent—mold. This does not mean either breaking with ASEAN or remaining aloof from Cambodia negotiations. On the contrary, close consultation and cooperation with the ASEAN countries remain imperative, as does direct involvement in the international peace process. But it means that the United States no longer has the luxury of a unified ASEAN policy on Cambodia which it can simply endorse.

The task of U.S. diplomacy will be to navigate the shoals of change and disagreement within the ASEAN group as their economies mature, as the effort to get a settlement in Cambodia continues (perhaps for years), and as ASEAN political relationships with Indochina unfold. In a real sense, ASEAN as an organization and its member states are suffering from success. There is no reason to believe that they will not handle these challenges with comparable ingenuity or that the United States cannot adapt to a more complex regional environment.

5

CHANGING TIMES

Indochina's internecine disputes are much like an oriental curio in which the tiny balls, carefully sculpted at the center of an ivory block, can move about but never escape, each one trapped by the others.[1] After 1978 this image of intractability and frustration applied perfectly to Cambodia, enmeshed simultaneously in the conflicting strategic interests of China and the Soviet Union and the historical enmities of its immediate Southeast Asian neighbors.

In the years immediately following the Vietnamese invasion, few in ASEAN or the world community expected an early resolution of the Cambodia problem. By the time of the UN International Conference on Kampuchea in July 1981, and certainly by June 1982 with the formation of the CGDK, the Cambodia stalemate seemed set in place indefinitely. In recognition of this stalemate and of the American inability to have much influence over the course of events, U.S. policy since the early 1980s has been summed up rather simply: "Let ASEAN take the lead on Cambodia."

While the Vietnamese persisted in their contention that the situation in Cambodia was irreversible, by the mid-1980s the winds of global political change and shifting interests within Southeast Asia began to create a new environment, one that would have an important impact on the Cambodia problem. Mikhail Gorbachev unveiled a fresh thrust for Soviet foreign policy. As early as 1982, Moscow and Beijing had commenced diplomatic foreplay aimed at ending 25 years of sour bilateral relations. ASEAN's rejection of "irreversibility" had caused Vietnam to rethink its position. At the same time, restlessness within ASEAN itself, particularly in the frontline state of Thailand, and internal developments in Vietnam and Cambodia were changing the perceptions of the regional players. While few observers in or

47

outside the region would then have proclaimed the beginning of the end of the stalemate in Cambodia,* events that took shape in the middle of the decade evolved during 1988–89 into the most promising opportunity yet for a resolution of the Cambodia problem. An important step in this process was the International Conference on Cambodia convened in Paris on July 30, 1989, and the organization of a multilateral forum to negotiate a political settlement.

In his Vladivostok address in July 1986, Gorbachev set out the grand lines of a new Soviet policy toward Asia and the Pacific basin. Although concentrating heavily on North Asia, where the Soviets place first strategic priority, the policy began to be fleshed out in Southeast Asia through an activist, culturally sophisticated Soviet diplomacy toward ASEAN and in adjustments of Soviet policies regarding Vietnam and Cambodia.

Gorbachev inherited from Brezhnev an implicitly coercive policy toward Southeast Asia that centered on the alliance with Vietnam as a means of projecting Soviet power, containing China, and countering the U.S. presence in the region in primarily military terms. The North Vietnamese victory in 1975 and the consummation of the mutual security treaty with Vietnam in 1978 confirmed this direction. Relations with ASEAN were deemed of minor value, partly because of the traditionally narrow Soviet outlook but also because the Soviet Union, quite accurately, felt economically and politically uncompetitive in Southeast Asia.

With Vladivostok, Gorbachev served notice of a more nuanced approach. The Soviet role became more than military, and attempts were made to erase the Soviet Union's boorish image by expressing eagerness for trade, economic contact, and greater

* An exception was Kishore Mahbubani, then deputy chief of mission at Singapore's Washington embassy (and later ambassador to the United Nations), who in early 1984 analyzed the weaknesses in Vietnam's position and rejected the notion of prolonged stalemate as being in neither Vietnam's nor ASEAN's interests. Mahbubani's outline of a negotiated settlement was remarkably close to what seemed to be emerging more than five years later. ("The Kampuchean Problem: A Southeast Asian Perception," *Foreign Affairs* (Winter 1983/84), pp. 407–25.)

political dialogue. This approach sought to erode U.S. strategic access to the region by exacerbating neutralist, antinuclear sentiment. While reaffirming the alliance with Vietnam, Moscow dangled hints that it would offer a "responsive gesture" on Cam Ranh Bay if the United States gave up its facilities in the Philippines.[2] The Soviet Union, in contrast to the United States, endorsed both SEANWFZ and the Treaty of Rarotonga, which declared a South Pacific nuclear weapons–free zone.

As of mid-1989, the Soviets had not added appreciable substance to their rhetoric, and many ASEAN leaders remained suspicious of their intentions in the region. The Soviets possessed neither hard currency to buy from nor products of interest to sell to ASEAN. But the Soviet Union had pledged support for a negotiated political settlement in Cambodia, and ASEAN was waiting to see if Moscow could obtain meaningful concessions from Vietnam on the fundamental issues involved.

Rapprochement with China was a second key element in the changes stirring in the mid-1980s. In Gorbachev's view, reduction of tensions in Asia was the underpinning for a successful *perestroika* at home and a consequent reversal of Soviet communism's decay. A summit meeting with Deng Xiaoping was the necessary stepping-stone. Several years of tough diplomatic negotiations on many fronts (including with the United States) culminated in 1988 with the onset of the withdrawal of the Soviet army from Afghanistan. During the same period the Soviets progressed toward settling their long-standing differences with China on border deployments. Thus two of Deng Xiaoping's three "obstacles" to better bilateral relations were removed. But the third obstacle, Cambodia, remained.

At Vladivostok (and in the July 1987 *Merdeka* interview), Gorbachev had declared the Soviet Union's intention to play an active role in breaking the Cambodia stalemate. By 1989 the Sino-Soviet discussions preparing the ground for a summit bore fruit. In February, Cambodia dominated the Beijing meeting of Soviet Foreign Minister Eduard Shevardnadze and his Chinese counterpart, Qian Qichen. Although disagreement remained on key points, China gained enough concessions, notably on a

September deadline for a Vietnamese withdrawal, to make the summit feasible. The nine-point communiqué, the first joint Sino-Soviet statement ever issued on Cambodia, outlined agreement on an effective control mechanism to supervise the Vietnamese withdrawal, on an end to outside military aid to the factions, on the holding of free elections at some point, on the removal of foreign troops or bases in Cambodia after a Vietnamese withdrawal, on an appropriate role for the UN, and on the convening of an international conference "when conditions are ripe."[3] Despite the ambiguities and differences papered over by these vague formulations, the historic Beijing meeting finally took place in May 1989, overshadowed ironically by the pro-democracy demonstrations in Tiananmen Square exhaustively reported by the international media on hand to see Gorbachev and Deng in action.

Movement toward a compromise on the Cambodian situation progressed in other areas as well. Vietnam, since 1982, had stated its intention to withdraw from Cambodia militarily "by 1990." Whether this meant January 1 or December 31, 1990, or perhaps earlier, was deliberately left murky by Foreign Minister Thach in his adroit media interviews and diplomatic discussions with ASEAN and western countries. From Hanoi's perspective of its own security needs, the PRK had to assume the defense burden before a withdrawal of the People's Army of Vietnam (PAVN) "volunteers" could take place safely. In 1982, the fledgling PRK's capability to defend its borders and maintain internal security was many years in the future.

Although the process of "Khmerization" held risks, military and security matters were only one aspect of a more complicated Khmer-Vietnamese relationship that, regardless of the ideological affinity and practical needs of the moment, was burdened by centuries-old ethnic and historical antagonisms. Speaking of the imperative to terminate the occupation, veteran Vietnamese diplomat Pham Binh, now ambassador to France, observed: "We recognize we have extremely sensitive relations with the Khmers. We cannot be short-sighted in this important matter. We cannot, and should not impose our will on the Khmers simply because they would hate us as before, in which case this generation might thank us but the next will hate us."[4] Vietnam had come to acknowledge the limits of its power (at least in the current stage of Indochina's history) in light of its grinding poverty and other problems at home.

Several well-publicized Vietnamese "troop withdrawals" between 1982 and 1986 were camouflaged unit rotations staged with much public relations hoopla but with little impact on overall combat levels. They tended to perpetuate international skepticism of Vietnam's real intentions. Beginning in late 1987 and through 1988, however, the Vietnamese did, in fact, bring home entire army units. The PAVN high command headquarters was removed to just across the border in Vietnam's Tay Ninh province, to the northwest of Ho Chi Minh City. Estimated total troop strength fell from a high of about 170,000 after 1979 (some analysts put the figure at 200,000) to approximately 120,000 during 1987, and to approximately 50,000–70,000 by the end of 1988.[5] At that point, the PRK used the term "three-quarters gone" in describing the status of the withdrawal.[6]

On April 5, 1989, Vietnam and the PRK, together with Laos, formally announced that "total withdrawal of Vietnamese volunteer forces from Kampuchea and the cessation of foreign interference, and of all foreign military aid to all Kampuchean parties must be achieved by the end of September 1989. . . . For her part, Vietnam will withdraw from Kampuchea all of her forces by the end of September 1989."[7] This joint declaration was the culmination of more than six years of diplomatic wrangling over a firm withdrawal timetable and the Vietnamese counterdemand of an aid cutoff to the CGDK resistance. So, just a few weeks before the Sino-Soviet summit, Vietnam had dropped its previous condition that a pullout in 1989 would occur only if an overall political settlement were reached ahead of time.

By pledging to deliver what China, ASEAN, and Vietnam's other opponents demanded—a timetable for getting out—Vietnam moved the Cambodia chess puzzle into the end game. Tactically, this move forced ASEAN's hand, as became clear just a few months later at the ASEAN foreign ministers' meeting. Many observers viewed the move as a deft Vietnamese diplomatic stroke. But Vietnam, making its independent assessment of reality, had already come to the conclusion to withdraw sooner rather than later for five major reasons.

Guerrilla harassment from the CGDK resistance, primarily the Khmer Rouge, was one, though by no means the most important, factor. Vietnamese soldiers in Cambodia lived to a large extent off the land; the Soviet Union funded fuel, arms, ammunition, and hardware costs. In direct economic terms the costs of occupation were tolerable, but the PAVN suffered steady casualties from the guerrilla fighting over the years (estimated 15,000 killed, 50,000 wounded) plus thousands more dead from malaria. As years went by, it became increasingly difficult to explain these losses back home. Without overestimating public opinion pressures in the Socialist Republic of Vietnam (SRV), it is fair to say that Hanoi felt the need to terminate the bleeding.*

The PAVN gained an important victory in the winter of 1984–85 when it destroyed the CGDK base camps along the Thai-Cambodian border. Yet no end to the insurgency was in sight so long as Thailand gave sanctuary and ASEAN and China provided material aid. "Vietnam's Vietnam" may overstate the case, but Hanoi realized the quagmire of a foreign army fighting an indigenous insurgency enjoying external support and a safe haven.

Second and more critical was economic pressure from ASEAN and the United States. Vietnam's mistaken Marxist policies and repressive political measures retarded its postwar reconstruction. "Basket case" or "shambles" accurately described Vietnam's economy. The Cambodian adventure exacerbated the already complex problems of shifting away from a wartime economy. As of mid-1989 Hanoi had in many respects not made this

* One of the bitter ironies of the third Indochina War is that many of the young Vietnamese recruits who died in Cambodia were the sons of South Vietnamese who fought in the armed forces of the Republic of Vietnam against the North in the second Indochina War. PAVN officers and noncoms were for the most part from the North.

shift. *Doi moi* or "renovation" (Vietnam's *perestroika*) made only fitful progress. Integration of the South into a socialist environment was delayed—indeed the South tended to go its own way more and more.

After 1986 Vietnam began to pursue a more rational economic approach under General Secretary Nguyen Van Linh and economic planner Vo Van Kiet. However, the isolation imposed by ASEAN, supported by the U.S. embargo and its blocking actions in the international financial institutions, severely hampered that effort. Japan, France, and the Asian Development Bank withheld or drastically scaled down aid programs. The modest operations of UNHCR and UNICEF did not meet Vietnam's need, and United Nations Development Programme (UNDP) and other international development agencies' activities were constrained because of the UN's political stance on the Vietnamese occupation. So while the involvement in Cambodia did not account directly for all Vietnam's ills, it nonetheless had a cumulative negative impact of major proportions throughout the decade.

Third, political pressure from ASEAN at the United Nations and elsewhere remained strong. Under astute ASEAN guidance, the lopsided vote in favor of keeping Cambodia's seat for the DK was sustained and grew year after year, in effect telling Vietnam that the world community, including much of the Non-Aligned Movement and many of Vietnam's friends on other issues, disapproved of the invasion and occupation. This no doubt came as a surprise to Vietnam, which had expected acceptance of the PRK after a decent interval; in 1979, Hanoi had not anticipated ASEAN's resourcefulness at the UN and elsewhere in world councils.

It was probably at the Sixth Party Congress of the Vietnamese Communist Party in December 1986 that Hanoi formally accepted a military exit from Cambodia—as soon as possible *before* 1990—as an essential precondition to ending its painful isolation.

Fourth, there was Soviet pressure. Western analysts can only guess how much comradely encouragement was offered to

Hanoi, but there is considerable circumstantial evidence. The thrust of the Soviet Union's East Asia policy since 1986 (including rapprochement with China), and pointed Soviet public statements about Vietnam's squandering of $10 billion in aid since 1975, left little doubt as to the message from Moscow. Preparatory negotiations for the May 1989 Sino-Soviet summit influenced Vietnamese deliberations, as Beijing persisted in its demand for a commitment by Vietnam to a precise withdrawal timetable, and Moscow made its preference for an early date increasingly plain. The Vietnamese could read the strategic tea leaves.

Fifth, Vietnam calculated that the PRK had, or would soon have, the capability to survive on its own with minimum direct Vietnamese assistance. All the other pressures taken together would probably have failed to persuade Hanoi to remove the PAVN had the bilateral arithmetic not added up to a reasonable chance for the PRK's survival. The PAVN shield had given the Kampuchean People's Revolutionary Armed Forces (KPRAF) time to organize, train, and gain confidence, and the Phnom Penh regime time to cultivate internal political and economic strength.[8] Still, it should be noted here that while the KPRAF's performance has reportedly improved significantly over the past year, as of summer 1989 its ability to stand up to the Khmer Rouge when the PAVN leaves remains open to question.[9]

By early 1989 the accumulation of pressures, several from external sources, left Vietnam little choice but to remove its military presence from Cambodia quickly. Yet Vietnam, after careful assessment of both the KPRAF's capability and the international political environment, had apparently already concluded on its own that the chance was worth taking. Divisions within ASEAN no doubt played a part in Hanoi's calculations, not the least being the actions of the new Thai government of Prime Minister Chatichai Choonhavan.

During the period 1986–88 ASEAN and Vietnam probed each other's conditions for ending the stalemate. It was Prince Sihanouk who, in his dynamic and unpredictable fashion, provoked a breakthrough that opened up negotiations on Cambodia. To the consternation of ASEAN and China, Sihanouk and his adversary, PRK Prime Minister Hun Sen, met near Paris in December 1987 in the first of a series of bilateral discussions. The two leaders agreed in principle that Cambodians, among themselves, should find some sort of accommodation; but they did not set a precise timetable for Vietnamese withdrawal, and they left other key issues unresolved. Among these were the dismantling of the PRK administration during the transition to a reconciliation government; the ground rules for writing a constitution and conducting elections; and the role—perhaps including that of peacekeeping—of an international supervisory and control body. The critical question of the future of the Khmer Rouge—still part of the CGDK and still generously supported by China—hovered over the bilateral talks. Sihanouk, carefully, did not burn his bridges with Beijing.

A second meeting between the two in January 1988 yielded no precise agreements but sketched out possible cooperative scenarios for a future settlement. Again the role of the Khmer Rouge, whose total exclusion Sihanouk said he would not accept, and a date for the Vietnamese withdrawal were prime sticking points. The initiation of a dialogue in these two meetings, however, represented a signal departure from previously frozen positions. They opened the possibility of a coalition between the noncommunist factions and the PRK—with the eventual exclusion or at least minimalization of the Khmer Rouge—and thereby touched the core issue of the Cambodia conundrum.

ASEAN, striving to control the Cambodia negotiating process and fearful of a Sihanouk–Hun Sen deal favorable to Vietnam, still faced the problem of the refusal of all the Cambodian parties, and of Vietnam, to talk directly with their opposition in a multilateral forum that might yield a comprehensive—as opposed to a partial—political settlement. In 1985, Malaysia had proposed "proximity talks" along the model of Afghanistan negotiations in order to get communication going in a setting where the political position of all parties could be reserved. Indonesian Foreign Minister Mochtar Kusumaatmadja pursued this concept for several years. In July 1988, eight months after the first Sihanouk–Hun Sen bilateral talks, Mochtar's successor, Ali Alatas, was able to arrange the ASEAN-sponsored Jakarta Informal Meeting (JIM), dubbed a "cocktail party" until Muslims objected.

In the hill station palace at Bogor, the CGDK leadership sat across the table from the PRK. Present were Hun Sen, Khieu Samphan (the "acceptable face" of the Khmer Rouge), the KPNLF's Son Sann, and Prince Sihanouk's son, Norodom Ranariddh of FUNCINPEC. In the wings as a "personal guest of President Suharto" was Sihanouk, on leave from the CGDK presidency in order to disassociate himself from the Khmer Rouge. Vietnam, Laos, and ASEAN representatives joined the meeting later. JIM made limited progress on substance, but the fact that the four parties had agreed to exchange views was in itself significant. Hun Sen put forward a seven-point proposal that dwelt on eliminating the Khmer Rouge leadership and asked Sihanouk to be head of a national reconciliation council. Summoning the four Cambodian representatives to the state guest house in Jakarta, Sihanouk announced he would drop insistence on an international peacekeeping force (IPKF) and would relax his earlier demand for dismantlement of the PRK governmental apparatus. The Khmer Rouge were totally negative, sensing that the momentum of the Sihanouk–Hun Sen relationship, despite deep and unbridged differences, was in the direction of a cooperation that, whatever form it took, would be hostile to them.

Beyond setting up a working group to prepare another meeting in 1989, no agreement was reached on a final JIM communiqué. The refusal of either Vietnam or the Khmer Rouge to alter its position was mainly responsible for JIM's limited success. The main beneficiary seemed to be Hun Sen, who came away with his prestige enhanced by implicit acceptance of the PRK as a party to multilateral Cambodia peace negotiations, however informal. Moreover, the Khmer Rouge's atrocities while in power, rather than the Vietnamese occupation of Cambodia, aroused the greatest international attention at Bogor, and this presented Vietnam a public relations victory.[10]

At the United Nations General Assembly a month later, the ASEAN Kampuchea Resolution became the focal point for unusual diplomatic maneuvering. Several factors contributed to a changed atmosphere: the JIM, the Sihanouk–Hun Sen discussions, and the international community's perception that 1989 could yield real progress toward a settlement. What persuaded ASEAN to revise the Kampuchea Resolution, which had carried easily with little change since 1979, was the international ground swell of revulsion at the prospect of a possible return to power of the genocidal Pol Pot regime.

The most controversial change put the General Assembly on record for the first time for "the non-return to the universally condemned policies and practices of a recent past," a thinly veiled reference to 1975–78. The Khmer Rouge and China mounted a hard-sell campaign on Third World delegates in an unsuccessful effort to defeat this provision. Reiterating the demand for Vietnam's withdrawal, the resolution included a new provision that it be conducted under the "effective supervision and control of an international commission," leaving open the question of whether this would be a UN force. It also noted the key role of Sihanouk "in the promotion of national reconciliation among all Kampucheans." The resolution, introduced annually for 10 years, carried in 1988 by its largest margin ever: 122 in favor, 19 against, with 13 abstentions.[11]

Reacting to ASEAN's pointed criticism, the Khmer Rouge boycotted the mid-October 1988 working group meeting in Jakarta preparing for "JIM 2." In November, Sihanouk and Son Sann met again with Hun Sen near Paris. In the face of Sihanouk's backing away from his compromise at JIM 1, Hun Sen hardened his position against any dismantlement of the PRK, and the parties could not agree on a firm timetable for Vietnam's withdrawal. Nonetheless, for the first time three of the four Cambodian parties (less the Khmer Rouge) signed a joint, if bland, communiqué. Moreover, the meeting contained the seeds of compromise in future negotiations that (though not foreseeable precisely at the time) would begin in the summer of 1989. The door was left open for Khmer Rouge attendance at future inter-Khmer meetings, an understanding that Sihanouk was careful to preserve in deference to China and to his own sense of what it would take to maximize his own position later on.

With these events as prologue, the first half of 1989 saw an unprecedented level of diplomatic activity among ASEAN, China, the Soviet Union, and Vietnam, each attempting to shape the chemistry of the evolving Cambodia situation in the direction of its own interests.

In a dramatic twist that challenged the basic unity of ASEAN's Cambodia strategy, Thai Prime Minister Chatichai invited Hun Sen to make a "private visit" to Thailand, January 25–26, 1989. A Royal Thai Air Force plane conveyed the 24-person PRK entourage from Vientiane to Bangkok for well-publicized meetings with Chatichai and leading Thai businessmen. Hun Sen did not come empty-handed. He promised to accept the voluntary repatriation of the 325,000 Cambodians in border camps, a neuralgic political issue for the Thai government. Sweetening the kitty, Hun Sen offered to open up Cambodia for Thai concessions in gemstone mining, lumbering, and fishing—all areas eyed with great interest by Thai entrepreneurs.

This gambit was part of Chatichai's determination, announced soon after he took office in early August 1988, to "turn Indochina from a battlefield into a marketplace." According to this strategy, Cambodia was part of a broader Indochina settlement that over time would integrate Vietnam into Southeast Asia. This concept was not novel: part of ASEAN's master plan since 1979 had been to use commerce and even economic aid as bait to coax Vietnam into a political settlement in Cambodia.

What *was* new—and to Thailand's ASEAN colleagues disturbing—was Chatichai's abrupt timing and unilateral departure from the long-standing policy of isolating the Phnom Penh regime *until* it and Vietnam showed unmistakable signs of compromise. ASEAN's trump card had been devalued, if not discarded entirely. The Thai prime minister had given Hun Sen and the PRK a valuable boost just before the second Jakarta Informal Meeting, slated for February 19–21, 1989. In addition, he had undercut Sihanouk and the CGDK at a delicate moment. The United States reportedly expressed its strong disapproval. Foreign Minister Sitthi Savetsila, who had visited Hanoi just two weeks earlier to discuss bilateral trade, and members of his Social Action Party were highly critical of the move. For their pains they were called "dinosaurs and million-year-old turtles" by Chatichai's followers. During the following weeks the Thai government backed away from officially embracing Hun Sen, but the impression had been planted that Thailand was ready to accept the PRK de facto and to do business right away—if Sihanouk could be brought into a coalition on minimally acceptable terms. Regardless of what their governments thought, other businessmen in the ASEAN countries were encouraged to follow suit.

It was hardly surprising that JIM 2 made no significant progress toward a settlement. Basking in the glow of his Bangkok conquest, Hun Sen was under less pressure to compromise with the CGDK on an interim quadripartite regime. Vietnam would not budge on its proposal for a limited (as opposed to UN-sponsored) international supervision of a complete withdrawal. With the Sino-Soviet summit less than three months away, none of the parties was inclined to yield ground on issues that would in any event have to be discussed in Moscow and Beijing. After JIM 2, many participants and observers believed that ASEAN's special format had outlived its usefulness, and that any successor multilateral forum would have to be an international conference with broader—and ultimately more authoritative—participation.

Sihanouk and Hun Sen met in Jakarta, on May 2, for their fourth round of talks amid speculation that they were moving closer to agreement on a coalition. With a flourish, Hun Sen announced a new name for the PRK—the "State of Cambodia" (SOC). A new flag, a new national anthem, and a new constitution had just been adopted in Phnom Penh. The constitution acknowledged Buddhism as the state religion and made other appealing gestures to Khmer traditions, but it also stipulated that the Kampuchean People's Revolutionary Party (KPRP) "is the leading force of the Cambodian society and state and the core force of the great national solidarity and unity of all political forces."[12]

Sihanouk stuck to his demand for inclusion of the Khmer Rouge in an interim government, and he rejected any constitution that failed to provide for a multiparty system. At the same time, he again modified demands for a peacekeeping presence and toned down his language on dismantlement of Hun Sen's apparatus prior to elections. Soon after this meeting, the Khmer Rouge, which had again refused to attend, announced its rejection of the cease-fire proposed by Thailand on May 6, and reiterated its insistence on complete dismantlement of the PRK. Sihanouk's NCR partner, Son Sann, backed the Khmer Rouge on this issue. In one sense the Cambodian parties were still far apart on the essentials. Yet the Sihanouk–Hun Sen dialogue was alive, and there were indications of a fairly broad agreement on many aspects of an eventual coalition between the noncommunists and the Phnom Penh administration. Sihanouk and Hun Sen scheduled another round of talks for late July in Paris, just prior to the international conference.

At the Sino-Soviet summit, May 15–18, 1989, Gorbachev and Deng continued to agree to disagree on specific details of a settlement, notably whether Hun Sen's government should remain in place during a transition. However, they reiterated the common ground on a general framework for a Cambodia settlement: prevention of civil war after a Vietnamese withdrawal, national reconciliation "with the participation of all four sides," elections under international supervision, gradual reduction of and eventual halt to external military aid to all the Cambodian parties, and the convocation of an international conference on Cambodia as soon as possible.[13]

The annual meeting of the ASEAN foreign ministers, held July 2–3 in Brunei, was followed by consultations with ASEAN's "dialogue partners" from five other countries, including the United States and the European Community. Cambodia headed the agenda. The Brunei meetings revealed the divisions within ASEAN regarding the proper tactics to follow at the international conference, scheduled to open on July 30, and even misgivings about holding a conference on such short notice with the prospect of a unilateral, unverified Vietnamese military withdrawal only a few weeks away. Reflecting anxiety over Thailand's overture to the PRK, Singapore's foreign minister said a settlement that left the Vietnam-installed regime in power in Phnom Penh "would make a mockery of ASEAN's ten years of solidarity and collective effort to undo the Vietnamese invasion of Kampuchea" and create "a dangerous precedent in Southeast Asia—a precedent that aggression pays."[14] ASEAN's final communiqué showed caution both in endorsing the Paris conference and in describing the Vietnamese announcement of a withdrawal by the end of September as a positive development. As ASEAN noted pointedly, the withdrawal would not be within the context of a comprehensive political settlement.[15]

6

END GAME IN CAMBODIA

For a decade, Cambodia's neighbors—ASEAN, particularly Thailand, Vietnam—had not suffered quite enough to throw in their hands and seek a negotiated political solution. During 1988, however, a consensus emerged that the costs of the Cambodia game exceeded the potential rewards. Consequently, in 1989 a political settlement in Cambodia, comprehensive or otherwise, appeared to be on the horizon. The "external aspects" of Cambodia's problems seemed near solution simply because the conflict's patrons, China and the Soviet Union, concluded that their broader interests would be better served by removing this regional irritation from their bilateral dialogue.

How to translate this possibility into the reality of a durable settlement had yet to be agreed upon either among the Cambodian factions or in Moscow, Beijing, Hanoi, and the ASEAN capitals, but with the convening in Paris of the international conference on Cambodia, the political momentum accelerated.

Concern remains widespread that Cambodia as a nation and a civilization may disappear if the current state of affairs continues, that it may become an Asian Lebanon doomed to perpetual self-mutilation. This fear contributes to the momentum to break the impasse. Statements by all four factions (we can take the Khmer Rouge's as less than sincere) express a desire for an end to the fighting and for some sort of reconciliation. After three decades of foreign intervention and the hideous Pol Pot years, the Cambodian people are certainly ready for peace.

The question is, are their leaders ready and what price are they prepared to pay? Despite external signs of change for the better, internal peace is *not* at hand, and it is entirely possible that Cambodia may slip into the agony of civil war. As yet there is no guarantee that the Vietnamese military withdrawal will be balanced by a cutoff of aid to the Khmer Rouge. China appears as suspicious as ever of Vietnam's ambitions in Indochina and of the Soviet-Vietnam alliance. Equally important, despite their fatigue and some progress toward accommodation, the four Cambodian factions have not resolved among themselves the internal aspects of a settlement—the future political, military, economic, and social shape of the country—nor the transitional arrangements necessary to achieve it.

How helpful will the outside patrons be in bringing the factions to heel? The communist great powers care less about the fate of Khmer civilization than they do about removing Cambodia as a source of regional friction and instability that delays pursuit of their own political and economic interests. Moreover, Moscow's capability and willingness to push Vietnam has limits. Many forces press Hanoi to agree to a settlement, yet Vietnam doggedly seeks a compromise shaped to the advantage of the PRK position on the ground.* The Khmer Rouge, militarily the most formidable internal faction, is the least susceptible to outside pressure, though it, too, must face the prospect of reduced material and human resources. The noncommunists, on the other hand, would appear to have little staying power on their own and rely almost totally on direct support from ASEAN and the United States.

Thus, unless Vietnam and China move more boldly toward compromise, the negative factors operating in and around Cambodia presage more strife and suffering for the Cambodian people.[1] The spring 1989 events in China have of course created additional grave uncertainties. Whether there will be progress toward peace or a continued slide toward civil war and another national disaster depends upon several basic questions.

- Will China, a major part of the problem, see it in its national interest to become part of the solution by agreeing to diminish and then cut off assistance to the Khmer Rouge?

- Will Vietnam and the PRK accept a Cambodia which is genuinely neutral in international affairs and relatively

* For simplicity, "PRK" rather than "SOC—formerly the PRK" is used in the following chapters.

open in its political system, or will they continue to work for a Cambodia dominated by a single party of Marxist-Leninist persuasion responsive to Vietnam?

- How much pressure will—or can—Moscow exert to move Vietnam and PRK toward compromise?

- Do ASEAN, the United States, and the West have the political will and the physical resources to gain a settlement closer to their own vision of a sovereign, neutral, independent Cambodia?

- Will China sequester the senior Khmer Rouge leadership in exile? Even if China is willing, will the Khmer Rouge leadership go quietly? If the remaining Khmer Rouge do not participate constructively in a coalition, will China and Thailand dispose of them or let them be eliminated in a protracted, bloody counterinsurgency campaign by a new Phnom Penh government?

- What, in the end, will Sihanouk accept as a reasonable compromise with respect to his own position in both a transitional and permanent government, and with respect to the role of the Khmer Rouge?

These are several plausible scenarios:

First, and the most terrible path for Cambodia, would be a return to power of the Khmer Rouge and a second round of genocide, with renewed destabilization of the region. Although many observers are convinced this could never happen, it is an eventuality that must be considered. What country or outside force, except possibly Vietnam, is prepared to stop the Khmer Rouge?

Second, the external powers would compromise or paper over the main external issues in order to move Cambodia to the regional back burner, and address the tough internal aspects only cosmetically. We are talking here not only about China and the Soviet Union but also about Thailand, which has historically used insurgencies on its borders for its own national purposes, and Vietnam, which has a variety of means short of outright military occupation to make its influence felt in Cambodia. Foreign military supplies would be reduced but not eliminated. The compromise would impose a settlement of convenience. It would protect the interests of the external powers, but would give short shrift to the aspirations of the Cambodian people and would not resolve the internal power issues. This outcome would guarantee continued violence and disruption with the threat that, willingly or not, the external parties might again be drawn in overtly.

Third, the negotiating process would break down and the present trend on the ground in Cambodia would be perpetuated—that is, there would be no settlement at all. The PRK, with continued help from Vietnam and the rest of the socialist bloc, would attain sufficient military power, *de facto* political authority and acquiescence in the populated areas of the country to battle the Khmer Rouge, perhaps for a period of years. Substantial assistance to the Khmer Rouge and noncommunists would continue. In effect, Vietnam and the PRK would attempt to make their fait accompli permanent, ASEAN and China would not acquiesce, and consequently there would be civil war.

Fourth, a quadripartite settlement involving *all* the Cambodian parties would be arranged, *including* the Khmer Rouge politically during the transition period but excluding their top leadership. There would be internationally supervised elections, a new constitution, several political parties, and eventually a new Cambodia, sovereign, nonaligned, and nonthreatening to either Vietnam or Thailand. At this point, such a scenario seems improbable. No one has devised a way to incorporate the "moderate" Khmer Rouge elements, assuming they exist, in a political settlement without potentially fatal risks. Whether this can be done at all even under the most favorable circumstances (including pressure from China) is doubtful. Yet there are important players in ASEAN, Thailand and Singapore principally, who are in favor of inclusion.

Fifth, a tripartite settlement excluding the Khmer Rouge entirely would be arranged. Sihanouk, Son Sann, and Hun Sen would share power. As in the fourth scenario, following a transition period, there would be internationally supervised elections, a new constitution, and two or more recognized political parties under Sihanouk and Son Sann in addition to Hun Sen's Kampuchean People's Revolutionary Party. ASEAN, the United States, the Soviet Union, Vietnam, and the rest of the international community would recognize and assist this coalition in the reconstruction of Cambodian society. Politically, Cambodia would be neutral and nonthreatening to any of its neighbors. A tripartite arrangement such as this might well perpetuate the Khmer Rouge insurgency and could even yield civil war. The outcome would depend on how well the Phnom Penh coalition held together, how effectively the international community could inject reconstruction assistance into the society, and perhaps most important to what extent the Khmer Rouge would continue to receive external support from China and safe haven in Thailand.

A "no-settlement solution" after Vietnam's military withdrawal would be risky for Hanoi as well as the PRK. The uncertainties include various anti-Vietnamese actions by China, continued support for the resistance, indefinite delay of normalization with the United States, and continued disapproval from ASEAN, all of which would cripple Vietnam's economic recovery. Civil war would gravely tax the PRK's capabilities.

Hanoi is making shrewd judgments here on what really matters to ASEAN, which for ten years has called for the removal of the Vietnamese military presence, not democracy or pluralism in Cambodia. ASEAN has proved that aggression by Vietnam will not be tolerated. Although most ASEAN leaders believe some sort of power-sharing is necessary to a stable Cambodia, democracy and humanitarian values are another matter. Between 1975 and 1978, ASEAN made no effort to remove Pol Pot from power. The horror might easily have continued years longer if the Khmer Rouge had not antagonized Vietnam so severely.

As for reintervention, Vietnamese Foreign Minister Thach says that "Kampuchea as a sovereign state has the right to ask again for Vietnam's assistance. But Vietnam would cede this privilege to those countries which have so far loudly demanded

Vietnam's withdrawal. Only in the case they decline their responsibility, shall we respond to the call of the Kampuchean people for help."[2] This approach would put ASEAN and the world community on the spot were the Khmer Rouge once again to threaten Phnom Penh. If history is any guide, Vietnam would do what is necessary to defend its border with Cambodia. This could mean military intervention as far west as Phnom Penh and a defensible line along the Mekong River and toward the Tonle Sap. But this time Hanoi would mount a well-orchestrated campaign for international backing, even military cooperation against the Khmer Rouge, and it could have some expectation of approbation rather than the condemnation of its earlier venture.

VIETNAM'S GOAL: PRESERVING THE ESSENCE OF PRK POWER

One can speculate that the majority of Cambodians who suffered under Pol Pot were grateful for Vietnam's removal of the Khmer Rouge from power, even if it required an invasion. But after ten years of military occupation, most Cambodians will be delighted to see the last PAVN unit depart. Mixed with this joy, however, is palpable anxiety among the people over the PRK's ability to defend them against the Khmer Rouge.

For Vietnam, preserving the PRK's assets and policy orientation, and the organizational sinews of the KPRP, is at the core of the negotiations. With the PAVN's departure, Vietnam is counting on ASEAN coming around to an acceptance of the present Phnom Penh regime—modified but with much the same character—as a basis for future stability in Cambodia. From Hanoi's perspective, "stability" means at minimum "no threat to Vietnamese security." Ideally, it would prefer a Cambodian regime "neutral" in favor of Vietnam and guided in critical affairs of state by a communist party whose primary international link is to Hanoi. Yet Hanoi may be willing to go along with pluralism if this would enhance reconstruction and stability in Cambodia and, hence, make for better security on Vietnam's border.

Hanoi is pursuing a two-track policy that allows for several of the different scenarios described above. It is gambling that the essential conditions for either the PRK's survival or its preeminence in a coalition environment can be put in place. The thrust of Vietnamese diplomacy in the next phase is to extract advantages strengthening, or at least preserving, this position. Vietnam believes time is on the PRK's side; the longer the PRK apparatus remains in control, the better the chances of lower-level political allegiances remaining reliable in a future coalition. The September 1989 deadline for troop withdrawal represents a compromise between what Vietnam probably wanted (late 1990) and what both circumstances at home and external factors forced it to accept. If the negotiations result in a coalition under Sihanouk, then Vietnam expects its interests will still be served by strong communist party-to-party and other internal bonds cultivated over the past decade.

With a timetable established, the next step in the international negotiating process is to make sure that the Vietnamese army actually leaves. How well the 1989 observation and verification procedures are carried out is critical to fitting together subsequent pieces of the settlement puzzle.

The record of the last quarter century inspires little confidence in Vietnam's fidelity to international agreements. Indochina is littered with the bones of failed coalition governments and broken accords. Cease-fire agreements and withdrawal promises have lasted only as long as the stronger party, which in most instances has been the communist party concerned, finds them useful. The histories of the International Control Commission in Laos after 1962 (ICC—India, Poland, and Canada) and the International Commission of Control and Supervision (ICCS—Hungary, Poland, Indonesia, and Canada) in Vietnam after the 1973 Paris Peace Accords are cases in point.[3]

It is not surprising, therefore, that ASEAN and China found Vietnam's original proposal for a reconstituted and slightly augmented ICC as the "international supervision" unacceptable from two perspectives. While the ICC might validate the PAVN's departure to the satisfaction of Vietnam's socialist bloc friends, small observer teams with only token arms and little authority would be inadequate to convince skeptics and helpless to prevent the Khmer Rouge from moving into the vacuum.

As this book is being prepared for publication, the terms of an observation, verification, and control agreement on the PAVN withdrawal that would satisfy all parties are being negotiated at the international conference in Paris. Without predicting the results of these negotiations, we can make several generalizations.

First, Vietnam's initial proposal may be disingenuous, but it has placed the burden for controlling the Khmer Rouge squarely on ASEAN, the West, and China, making them responsible for cutting off external assistance. If they fail to respond, ASEAN (principally Thailand) and China would be held accountable in the eyes of the world for a Khmer Rouge resurgence. Moreover, ASEAN will have to face the consequences of its pact with the devil sooner rather than later: If the Khmer Rouge do not become part of the reconciliation process, then ASEAN and China must find some effective means of isolating them to wither on the vine or destroying them outright. Either option is formidable. Meanwhile, Hanoi and the PRK will attempt to deny the charge of total intransigence.

Second, whatever the nature of outside observation, Vietnam would like maximum opportunity to pass on elements of military advantage to its ally. China and Sihanouk have charged that a considerable number of Vietnamese soldiers have already shed their PAVN uniforms and been absorbed into PRK army units. Though unconfirmed, this issue will certainly receive attention, as will the question of PAVN advisers remaining with the KPRAF in the field. As for elite PAVN strike forces that Hanoi might want to keep in-country, the jungles of eastern Cambodia offer secluded base areas; they have been tracked by the Vietnamese for decades and would be difficult to police by outside observers. High-resolution aerial photography and infrared and other sophisticated sensing techniques make the border monitoring task easier, but detecting "advisers" and small units would be extremely difficult. On the other hand, major Vietnamese units, regular or irregular, could not easily operate clandestinely in central and western Cambodia, where much of the fighting would probably occur.

Third, and perhaps most important, ASEAN, China, the United States, and the rest of the world community that has criticized the invasion and occupation must be convinced that the withdrawal conforms with terms set down in negotiations. If they are not convinced, Vietnam loses its political and economic pay-off. Normalization, trade, and access to international financial institutions would not follow automatically. These are the "goods" Hanoi must receive as a result of a Cambodia settlement.

Vietnam's interests dictate that the withdrawal be credible to the international community. This imperative may eventually drive Vietnam to accept a leading role by the United Nations in administering the observation process rather than by a weak ICC. The September withdrawal of PAVN is not an event with a terminal date; it is an integral part of the overall Cambodia settlement that will require continual monitoring.

How to deal with the Khmer Rouge, immediately and in a future settlement, remains at the heart of the Cambodia problem. The Khmer Rouge must be prevented from moving into the vacuum created by Vietnam's departure. At this point, in the wake of the spring 1989 political events in China, Beijing's attitude toward the Cambodia problem is unclear. But without a coalition agreement, once the PAVN units depart, the PRK armed forces will essentially stand alone. While this may present short-term opportunities for the Armee Nationale Sihanoukiste (ANS) and KPNLF, the Khmer Rouge will have a far greater capability to expand their influence and perhaps control some areas along the Thai border and outside of their bases in the Cardamom Mountains. Conceivably, they could mass enough muscle to occupy some provincial capitals and even threaten Phnom Penh itself.

Thus, for ASEAN and other opponents of the Vietnamese presence in Cambodia, certain consequences of the PAVN's departure, which few observers thought would take place before

1990, are frightening. The immediate political challenge is at the negotiating table, but the enduring determination of the Khmer Rouge to regain power and their military capability are the core problems. At the July 1989 ASEAN ministerials, not a few senior leaders expressed concern that Vietnam's army was leaving Cambodia too soon!

Some analysts speculate that the Khmer Rouge has split into internal factions, and that traditional "warlordism" and a preoccupation with money-making activities (smuggling, gem mining, logging) on the border have sapped its vitality. Morale is said to be low and recruitment difficult. DK Foreign Minister Khieu Samphan is portrayed as leader of a "moderate" wing in opposition to Pol Pot and his closest henchman, Ta Mok. Rivalry reportedly broke the unity of the army.[4] These rumors remain speculative.

The Khmer Rouge camps along the Thai border are still ruled with the draconian discipline of 1975–78. Conditions there are characterized by intimidation, outright terror, and the absence of any semblance of human rights.[5] Civilians are impressed as porters on dangerous routes into the Cambodian interior; hundreds have reportedly lost their lives in such service. Movement of any sort is strictly regulated; the camps themselves are, for all intents and purposes, prisons, since exit is forbidden. In the summer and fall of 1988, the Khmer Rouge forcibly removed an estimated 16,000 refugees from O'Trao and Ta Luan refugee camps and marched them into the interior for resettlement as "the vanguard of the new revolution."[6] In mid-1989, international aid agencies reported that 4,000 Cambodian civilians were abducted from Ta Luan and taken somewhere into "liberated zones."[7] Access to camps by foreigners, including the UN Border Relief Organization (UNBRO) and the Office of the UN High Commissioner for Refugees, is possible only under conditions dictated by the Khmer Rouge for propaganda purposes.

Thanks to the Chinese, the Khmer Rouge have reportedly amassed stockpiles of weapons and supplies inside Cambodia in preparation for a cease-fire and a cutoff of external assistance.

Thus even without further resupply, the Khmer Rouge could go it alone for a year or more at a fairly high level of military activity.

Estimates of the Khmer Rouge's military strength vary. Much depends on definitions: "armed regulars," "main force," village militia, support troops, political versus military cadres. Some observers claim that the effective strength is only somewhere between 8,000 and 15,000.[8] Other estimates put the effectives at 23 brigades with 20,000 men, and growing. The ASEAN and U.S. intelligence community consensus seems to be 30,000 to 40,000 "armed men," however one defines that term.[9] One important distinction that must be made is between hard-core "old Khmer Rouge," that is the cadres who date back to 1975–79, and recent recruits 12 to 20 years old. The former may number no more than 10,000 but are judged fanatically committed ideologically and loyal to Pol Pot, who is said to be in retirement (but still giving orders) near Trat in extreme southeast Thailand. It is along this strip of land between the Gulf of Thailand and the Cardamom Mountains that dozens of Khmer Rouge military and civilian camps are located.[10] It is worth remembering that when Pol Pot overwhelmed the Lon Nol army in 1975, his force of 30,000 had a high percentage of fighters in their early teens.

Though observers may differ as to precise numbers, they agree that the elite Khmer Rouge forces are well equipped, highly trained and disciplined, and superior in fighting capability, unit-for-unit, to the other factions.

While the Khmer Rouge have tried to display a benign image, even preaching liberal democracy, and have purposely kept their military activity at a low level, there is no reason to believe that Pol Pot's men have lost any of their deadly zeal or determination to dominate Cambodian life. On the contrary, in early 1988 a defector from Ta Mok's command made available a Khmer Rouge training manual, dated December 2, 1986, that lays out in stark detail the plan to reconquer Cambodia using a combination of propaganda, cadre proselytizing, deceit, and brute force. It makes clear that the enemies are not only the Vietnamese and the PRK but also the two noncommunist factions in the CGDK.[11]

THE PRK's BIGGEST ASSET—MEMORIES OF POL POT

KNUFNS veterans of the 1979 blitzkrieg that deposed Pol Pot form the backbone of the regime in power in Phnom Penh. They also dominate the ruling Kampuchean People's Revolutionary Party and its "mass organizations." Hun Sen, the prime minister and most visible figure, came from a peasant family and was in secondary school in Phnom Penh when Lon Nol overthrew Sihanouk in 1970. He joined the Khmer Rouge at the age of eighteen and rose to become a senior military commander in the Eastern Zone. In July 1977 he defected to Vietnam to escape the purge of suspected pro-Vietnamese cadres. He is said to have been in positions of authority during the worst years of the Khmer Rouge slaughters, 1975 to 1977, although no details of his precise responsibility are known.

Returning with the Vietnamese in 1979, he became one of the world's youngest foreign ministers. He was appointed chairman of the PRK council of ministers in 1985. To some foreign observers, Hun Sen appears to be building a cult of personality, so omnipresent are his pictures and media references. He seems to eclipse Heng Samrin, the head of state, but no Westerner can know certainly how power flows today in Cambodia. It is surmised that Hun Sen shares power with not only Heng Samrin but Chea Sim, leader of the national assembly and senior KPRP ideologue, and with other less well-known KNUFNS veterans.

With memories of Pol Pot still fresh, Cambodians are suspicious of any ideology or government. The PRK's human rights abuses, especially in its early years, and its heavy-handed rule have probably not endeared the regime to the population.[12] Cambodians profoundly distrust, indeed often hate, the Vietnamese. Moreover, the Solidarity Front for the Liberation of Kampuchea captured Phnom Penh only thanks to Vietnam and has been kept in power through a Vietnamese occupation that most Cambodians want ended despite their fear of Pol Pot. Still, the Front did replace Pol Pot, and one can speculate that the Cambodian people judge the PRK's governance against their earlier experiences of mass murder and slavery. Western observers and overseas Khmer who have traveled widely in Cambodia believe that comparison reflects favorably on the current regime.

The PRK, with help from Vietnam and the socialist bloc, has created a political base. It has provided a skeleton organization upon which individuals and groups are rebuilding their lives. Its infrastructure of administrative services and economic organization functions in Phnom Penh and the larger provincial centers. According to foreign voluntary agency representatives who travel outside Phnom Penh, government services in rural areas, though still weak, are improving. The regime's resources are extremely limited, consisting of a handful of experienced administrators and professionals (doctors, engineers, technicians) in any given province. These persons operate on a tiny budget with little equipment or supplies. At the same time, cadres of the KPRP have been trying to install information and education networks. Despite the suspicion of ideology, these activities will work in favor of the KPRP in future political contests.

No one can predict how durable any part of the PRK infrastructure would be if seriously challenged by force of arms or at the ballot box by Sihanouk and Son Sann. Nor can outsiders accurately judge how much genuine "rice-roots" support the PRK has been able to generate. The government has mounted a major organizational and motivational effort in the past two or three years, and it feels confident enough of the people's allegiance to hand out an estimated 60,000 small arms to village self-defense militia.

One must look back to 1979 for perspective. For all its abuses, lack of resources, and structural weaknesses the PRK administration exists. At this point in Cambodia's history, existence counts for a lot. The population's memory of Pol Pot is the PRK's strongest asset.

Also significant are economic changes under the PRK—perhaps the trashing of socialism would be a more accurate description. The regime evidently operates on the theory that power grows from the pocketbook as well as out of the barrel of the gun. Phnom Penh, home to approximately 700,000 people (about 10 percent of the country's population), is experiencing a mini-boom in commercial activity, construction, and refurbishing of neighborhoods decaying since 1975. With its streams of bicycles and motorcycles, bustling markets and shops stocked with goods from Singapore, Thailand, and Japan, as well as from Vietnam and Laos, Phnom Penh looks more like entrepreneurial, freewheeling Ho Chi Minh City than the decaying, provincial Hanoi. Travelers to other towns report comparable economic activity and the prevalence of private commercial enterprise. In the agricultural sector, the *krom samaki*, or "solidarity work group," resembles traditional Cambodian community-based rice cultivation practices. The government has used incentives and other free market tools to increase production to a far greater extent than Vietnam has dared. Against the dollar, the Cambodian riel inflated only 10 percent in 1988 (compared with 1,000 percent for the Vietnamese dong). In the first half of 1989, however, the official exchange rate of the riel weakened considerably against the black market in reaction to uncertainty surrounding peace negotiations.[13]

While Cambodia remains one of the world's most impoverished countries, improvements have been made over the last five years starting from essentially a zero level. The reason: The socialist PRK has used a pragmatic, nonideological approach to reconstruction, including a free market philosophy and permissive land tenure and property ownership policies. Cambodian officials show open contempt for Vietnam's economic mess and vow never to follow big brother's example. ("We will never make all their mistakes; we've seen firsthand under Pol Pot that socialism doesn't work," one senior official has observed to the author.[14]) Western-trained economic advisors (Kom Somol and Kong Keng, both ministerial level economists, and Uch Kiman, a former Lon Nol diplomat with experience in Australia and the United States) preach the message that the private sector and free market forces are the path to quick recovery in Cambodia. Perhaps somewhere in Phnom Penh there is a shrine where state socialism is preserved pure and pristine for the day when Cambodia is prosperous and the private sector can be peremptorily

most are not really sure what the Prince's FUNCINPEC or Son Sann's KPNLF represent, how their presence would affect the economy, or how they could protect the country against the Khmer Rouge.[19] But people are painting their homes and shops, and thereby declaring hope for the future—a few years earlier this sort of investment was rare.

These summary impressions are subjective and limited, of course, but one conclusion is inescapable: the commercial hustle and bustle in Phnom Penh's bazaars and the gradual rise in food production because of market incentives are of direct significance to the negotiating process for the political future of Cambodia. For now, the pace and direction of that economic activity is controlled by Hun Sen and the PRK.

It is not necessary to praise Hun Sen's economic pragmatism but only to recognize that through the marketplace he is building a situation of strength against the ANS and the KPNLF, and of course the Khmer Rouge. This is a reality, not a moral judgment. The PRK, under clever leadership, is creating political capital through economic reconstruction. Put simply, Hun Sen is courting Cambodians who want a better life on the free enterprise turf. When Cambodians ask themselves, "Under whose leadership do I stand a better chance of buying a bicycle," Hun Sen is betting that in an election a majority will vote for the KPRP. FUNCINPEC and the KPNLF will have to make a case that they can provide greater economic resources and offer greater hope for prosperity, while preserving security.

Politically, Hun Sen is sending a not so subtle message: a settlement can only come if Sihanouk and Son Sann accept his terms, at least with respect to the nonparticipation of the Khmer Rouge in an interim government and integration of the defense establishment. Negotiations for reconciliation are to a large extent taking place on Hun Sen's turf—the balance of forces on the ground leaves his challengers no choice. On the other hand, Hun Sen acknowledges mutual compromises will be required. Both sides have made concessions—this is what the bilateral meetings were about. Meanwhile, the political use of economic liberalization has added a dimension to the struggle for power that few observers would have anticipated two or three years previously.

What military assets do Sihanouk and Son Sann—the non-communist resistance—have to defend themselves against the Khmer Rouge and, if need be, to challenge Hun Sen? Sihanouk's ANS claims an effective troop strength of 18,000.[20] The Bush administration has made known its intention to help increase that number to 30,000 or more by the end of 1989. Assessments vary as to its fighting capability; knowledgeable observers consider some ANS units to be well trained, motivated, adequately equipped for guerrilla combat, and well led. The ANS operates mostly in north-central Cambodia from bases along the Thai-Cambodian border. Its emphasis has been on political activity in the interior, but it has occasionally engaged Vietnamese forces. In recent years there has been a significant degree of accommodation, if not cooperation, between the ANS and the PRK's armed forces. The ANS claims substantial results in attracting defectors; the PRK makes reverse claims. In reality, a lively two-way defector traffic probably exists among the lower ranks of both sides. The ANS considers the Khmer Rouge its prime enemy, and during 1989 there were many fire fights between the two "allies."

The KPNLF claims 12,000 effectives, but this is probably an inflated figure. The Bush administration has also made known plans to help increase the KPNLF's numerical strength. Whatever the numbers, the KPNLF has been judged a negligible military force in recent years. A prolonged leadership crisis has pitted Son Sann against his armed forces commander, General Sak Sutsakhan. Whatever modest capabilities the force possessed in the early 1980s have been eroded by corruption, black marketeering, and petty power squabbles among its commanders. The Pentagon's polite assessment: "The KPNLF lacks the coherent planning and organization of the ANS. Its operations consist of shallow, small-scale penetrations of northwestern Cambodia."[21] In 1989 the KPNLF reportedly pulled itself together somewhat; perhaps this effort will be spurred by the challenge of an imminent settlement.[22] Many observers believe, however, that the KPNLF could become a military factor only if it operated jointly with the ANS and only if its grievous leadership problems were resolved.

ASEAN has been the main supplier of arms and equipment for the Cambodian noncommunist resistance since 1982, with China providing lesser quantities. There have been reports that China has begun to channel a large flow of supplies to the NCR. As noted in Chapter 4, the United States has overtly supported Sihanouk and Son Sann since fiscal year 1985 at an annual rate of about $3.5 million through the Solarz program (medical supplies, malaria prevention, training, and commodities), and since fiscal year 1989 additionally through the McCollum program providing excess Department of Defense stocks (nonlethal) and administrative and transportation expenses. In fiscal year 1989, the administration requested $5 million and $0.5 million, respectively, for these programs. In March 1989, the Solarz program request was boosted to $7 million, "in preparation for a settlement in Cambodia and to strengthen the noncommunist resistance to help prevent the return of the Khmer Rouge to power."[23]

The administration has continued to review assistance levels in the light of developments in the negotiations. The focus since March 1989 has been on a substantial dollar increase and, for the first time, lethal assistance. Representative Solarz has again been a vigorous proponent, arguing first that the noncommunists must be given the military capability to protect themselves against the Khmer Rouge in the likely event of civil war and, second, that Sihanouk must have a stronger hand to play at the negotiating table. In Solarz's words, "A decision to provide lethal assistance to the NCR would enhance the prospects for a political settlement by sending a signal to Vietnam and the PRK that we are not about to accept the Hun Sen regime as an accomplished fact."[24]

Following his visit to Southeast Asia in May 1989, Vice President J. Danforth Quayle has emerged as the administration's senior spokesman on aid to the noncommunist factions. In Jakarta, he met with Prince Sihanouk on the occasion of the fourth bilateral discussion with Hun Sen and declared U.S. support for Sihanouk in a coalition. In Bangkok, the vice president had talks with the Thai government on Cambodia and toured resistance camps on the border. In his June 22, 1989, speech at the Heritage Foundation, Quayle set out the administration's determination to build up the NCR, saying ". . . we have a compelling moral responsibility to do what we can, short of direct intervention, to provide the wherewithal for the Cambodian people to have a genuine choice in determining their future." The purpose of lethal aid, he said, was ". . . to make it possible for him [Sihanouk] to be *independent* of the Khmer Rouge *without* becoming a prisoner of the Vietnamese-sponsored puppet government."[25] (Emphasis in speech.)

After lengthy debate, the U.S. Senate on July 20, 1989, on the eve of the Paris conference, approved an amendment (by Senator Charles Robb, D.-VA) to the State Department's authorization bill, which expressed the Senate's support for lethal aid to the NCR and gave the president this option. Similar legislation was passed in the House. The Senate's Democratic leadership, however, remained opposed to lethal aid, and the Robb amendment did not assure its future provision, either overtly or convertly.

The international community is finally coming to grips with the fundamental issues of transition to a political settlement, as soon as the Vietnamese army departs Cambodia. A number of vital questions must be addressed: inclusion or exclusion of the Khmer Rouge, peacekeeping, elections, the UN role, forms of support for the noncommunists, reconstruction assistance for Cambodia, and the complicated and expensive technical problems associated with all these activities. The results of the ASEAN ministerial meetings in Brunei and international conference in Paris indicate that the Bush administration is actively involved in this effort. Beyond provision of more assistance to the NCR, the basic questions are: how much influence does the United States—after years of relative passivity—actually have in this complicated multilateral setting; and how much political will is it willing to dedicate to securing a comprehensive settlement that endures?

7

CHALLENGES FOR U.S. POLICY

The Bush administration inherited from its predecessors a Cambodia policy that was cautious, passive, and reactive to the inclinations of ASEAN and China. Through Thailand, the Reagan administration provided financial support to the NCR, and permitted the Thai and others to carry out the actual organization, sustenance, and strengthening of the resistance forces. By standing at one remove from the dirty business of insurgency, the United States had little ability to shape the military or political efficacy of the NCR; during the early and mid-1980s, this seemed perfectly agreeable to U.S. interests.

A number of reasons account for this recessive posture: extraordinary sensitivity in Congress and the media about "another Vietnam," the sincere conviction that ASEAN should carry the ball, the fact that the Thai army was in charge on the ground, a visceral reluctance on the part of the American bureaucracy to jump back into Indochina, and the disinclination to interfere in an affair of particular interest to China. But regardless of this hands-off attitude, its status as a superpower, its rhetorical support for the NCR and ASEAN, as well as its funding, made the United States a player. In the end, the United States may have have gotten the worst of both worlds—a gradual political commitment to an involvement without being able to shape its eventual dimensions.

The Reagan administration did not take into account the long lead time needed to prepare the NCR for participation in a negotiated political settlement. Until 1987 negotiations seemed a long way off. The administration turned a blind eye to the implications of the residual power of the Khmer Rouge. When the stalemate showed signs of breaking, it seemed reluctant to discuss with ASEAN—most importantly, Thailand—measures to curb the Khmer Rouge. More interested in strengthening the

82

"strategic relationship" with China, the Reagan administration declined to make the future of Cambodia and the fate of the Khmer Rouge front rank issues in the bilateral dialogue with Beijing.

Goaded by congressional and public realization that the Khmer Rouge still posed a threat, and because of movement toward negotiations, the Bush administration began to address the Cambodia issue soon after taking office in 1989. In preparation for the July ASEAN ministerial conference, the administration formulated general requirements of a settlement: a verified and complete withdrawal of all Vietnamese military forces, effective safeguards against the return to power of the Khmer Rouge, and genuine self-determination for the Cambodian people.

The administration has placed its weight behind the concept of "an interim coalition government under Prince Sihanouk which will lead to free elections and genuine stability in Cambodia, and prevent the return to the Khmer Rouge 'killing fields.'" It intends to strengthen the NCR "in as many ways as possible . . . to increase the political strength of the Noncommunist Resistance in the peace process while simultaneously giving it the strength to hold its own in the event of a Khmer Rouge attempt to seize power."[1]

This statement leaves open fundamental questions about how deeply the United States intends to become involved in the process of a peace settlement, and what commitment it would be willing to make in order to ensure a pluralist form of government. Preventing the Khmer Rouge from returning to power is a clear enough primary goal, but there remains ambiguity—if not confusion—on other crucial aspects of Cambodia policy. *If* the PAVN departs Cambodia and *if* the Khmer Rouge can be prevented from regaining power, is the United States prepared to deal with a regime in Phnom Penh that remains tainted by its origins in the Vietnamese occupation and Khmer Rouge presence?

Statements by the secretary of state at the Brunei meetings indicate that the United States would be prepared to support a government in which the PRK has an important, if not leading, role. Some observers believe Hun Sen's State of Cambodia might have a fair chance of evolving into a rather odd sort of communism, basically free market and private enterprise economically and something less than totalitarian politically. A parallel could be drawn between what is happening currently in Poland and Hungary and what we would hope to see evolve in a future Cambodia. Other observers are skeptical for reasons cited in the previous chapter. This has created a new round of controversy over the nature and feasibility of American objectives.[2] The dilemma remains: How committed is the United States to seeking both objectives in a future Cambodia—no Khmer Rouge return to power and a semblance of democracy or pluralism?

In 1982, ASEAN's intent in sponsoring the formation of the CGDK was to create pressure on Vietnam. China, with U.S. acquiescence, poured resources into the Khmer Rouge. The idea was not to defeat Vietnam militarily but to make the CGDK strong enough to drive Vietnam to the negotiating table for a political solution. Guerrilla warfare was only one of several pressures. The noncommunists under Sihanouk and Son Sann, it was hoped, would become strong enough to hold their own, whether or not they were ever able to dominate the CGDK and take the political lead in a future government. There was no indication during the mid-1980s that the United States intended to become directly involved in such an effort. The Khmer Rouge were to be the military cutting edge. Little thought was given by the administration to the problem of disposing of the Khmer Rouge when negotiating time came—that was a job for others.

ASEAN never did what was necessary to make the NCR genuine contenders either militarily or politically simply because peace negotiations seemed far in the future. Moreover, the NCR was apparently not thought of as a genuine political alternative in a future Phnom Penh government. Two Reagan administrations either did not understand or simply ignored the NCR and its possible role in a future Cambodian body politic. Perhaps this was the real reason why Representative Solarz's rather modest program for training for the more than 300,000 Khmer refugees languishing in camps in Thailand caused such trouble for the Reagan administration: it raised the fundamental issue of "where do we go from here?"—no one wanted to find the answer to this question. Thus money was provided covertly (and after 1985 overtly) but the tough political questions—organization, leadership, motivation, and the NCR's *objectives*—were not addressed. The NCR leaders were divided among themselves and unsure of either their foreign supporters or their own purposes. Moreover, they lacked motivation and professional competence and in many cases were dishonest. Basically, most of eight years were wasted.

The Khmer Rouge, meanwhile, with lavish Chinese support and Thai protection, rebuilt their military capability while using Sihanouk, Son Sann, and the CGDK as a cloak of international respectability. And the PRK continued its own growth process (in effect nation-building) with ample Vietnamese and Soviet aid and advice.

The Bush administration, consequently, has been placed in the predicament of espousing public support for a political entity, the NCR, which has little capability to defend itself either militarily or politically, in a rough-and-tumble fight, or so it appeared in the relatively early stages of the Paris conference. Two Cambodian-American community leaders testified at a March 1989 congressional hearing that "the NCR forces are totally unprepared to deal with a speedy settlement of the Cambodian question. . . . If a compromise settlement were to take effect today, we would find forces of Prince Sihanouk and the KPNLF [Son Sann] incoherently scrambling to try to take hold of the situation, without much of a cohesive strategy and tactics, militarily weak, lacking adequate administrative structure, and without a political organization firmly entrenched inside Cambodia."[3]

In Congress and in the media, proponents of lethal assistance to the noncommunists squabbled with those who would deny any aid by law unless Sihanouk breaks his ties to the Khmer Rouge. The Pell amendment to the State authorization bill in the Senate that put forward this view was ultimately tabled.[4] The choices seemed to be *either* to throw weapons at the problem at a very late date *or* to prohibit any aid and dictate Sihanouk's negotiating strategy. Putting the argument in such black and white terms has hindered finding a way to help the non-communists in their struggle to survive in a future Cambodian government.

Whatever the shortcomings of past policies, with the Cambodia end game moving forward the Bush administration must work with what it has and choose carefully what additional measures it wishes to adopt. The United States is not without assets in this complex situation, and it can pursue a more active Cambodia policy without being trapped in that much feared Indochina quagmire. The emphasis should be upon multilateral diplomacy, international cooperation, and use of the tools already at our disposal.

The points below illuminate some of the policy choices that the United States faces today and suggest where we should stand on the essential elements of a Cambodia settlement.

INCLUSION OF THE KHMER ROUGE IN A POLITICAL SETTLEMENT

The transition to a political settlement after a Vietnamese withdrawal remains a key issue. The Chinese attitude is critical, and the extent to which the recent events in China will affect its policy on Cambodia is unknown. Some analysts believe Beijing, in its current mood, will return to intransigence in regional affairs, continue to "bleed" Vietnam, and keep open the supply line to the Khmer Rouge—or even cheer them on. Others believe that a certain sober momentum in Chinese foreign policy and cooler bureaucratic heads may prevail. Preoccupied with internal matters, Beijing may be willing to drop odious enterprises of marginal value, like the Khmer Rouge, and will curry favor with ASEAN by winding down the Cambodia affair. Just how the spring 1989 events will ultimately affect Sino-Vietnamese normalization is also uncertain.

We do know that China has favored the creation of a "provisional coalition government" headed by Sihanouk with the par-

ticipation of all four factions. This would require the dismantlement of the PRK structure and relegation of Hun Sen to being
head of one faction within a superior and temporary ruling
body. The Khmer Rouge have reiterated their maximum demand on this point.

The Soviet Union also wants the creation of a provisional
body, but of a quite different nature. The PRK would continue to
govern Cambodia, while the provisional body, headed by
Sihanouk and with representatives of the four Cambodian factions, would carry out agreements reached by those four factions
on the holding of elections and would decide on future steps
toward a new constitution and a government incorporating, it is
presumed, all factions.

The core problem, however, remains the disposition of the
Khmer Rouge—both politically and militarily—either in a transition period or in the final settlement itself. This is what the
arguments over a tripartite versus a quadripartite regime are all
about, whether it is better to have the Khmer Rouge spitting in
the tent or spitting into the tent from outside.

The transition period, which could be from several months
to two years or more, is critical because whoever administers the
daily life of the country will be able to influence the preelection
environment. The Khmer Rouge, were they part of the provisional coalition government, would have an increased capability
for disruption and conceivably could wreck what stability now
exists. Similarly the PRK, were it to retain day-to-day governing
authority, would hold an advantage. In any event FUNCINPEC
and the KPNLF will have an uphill battle to organize their
political networks and to make their programs known to the
populace. Just surviving may be a full-time task.

It is all but certain that the Khmer Rouge will eventually end
up as insurgents regardless of what type of regime is organized
initially in Phnom Penh as a result of the Paris negotiations. If
China makes good on its pledge to reduce or eliminate support
for the Khmer Rouge as Vietnam departs, then peace might be
possible—but only after more fighting to subdue the Khmer
Rouge in a long counterinsurgency operation. Thailand's deter-

mination to deny sanctuary to the Khmer Rouge and to take casualties along the border in enforcing this decision is crucial.

An all-out offensive by the Khmer Rouge to capture Phnom Penh and other main population centers cannot be excluded. It seems more likely, however, that the Khmer Rouge would pursue a two-track policy combining coercion and legitimate politics, designed to maintain a thread of support and protection from China and Thailand. In a quadripartite interim arrangement, certain cadres would participate legally in preparations for elections and other affairs of state, establishing themselves in key positions and building strength within the system. These legal participants, the benign Khmer Rouge with, perhaps, Khieu Samphan as their leader, would follow this legal route only so far as it served the purpose of moving closer to their ultimate goal of exclusive power.

Simultaneously, Khmer Rouge military units in the jungles and the Cardamom Mountains that were disassociated from the "legals" in Phnom Penh would attempt to destabilize the central government through insurgency, in preparation for the day when a full-scale military offensive could succeed. Terror and intimidation would be used selectively. There would be clandestine coordination between these inside-outside groups.

Assuming the quadripartite arrangement, a major uncertainty would be the disposition of the senior leadership: Pol Pot, Ieng Sary, Ta Mok, Son Sen, plus several others and their wives. China has not publicly offered asylum; Reagan administration officials claimed they had tacit assurance that the Chinese "would take care of things." But no promises have been made, let alone kept.[5]

Sihanouk has designed his strategy to appeal to China. He wants to go as far as possible toward inviting the Khmer Rouge inside the tent, at least in the interim period, for three reasons. First, unless China renounces the Khmer Rouge as an organization, their inclusion initially in a quadripartite arrangement seems in practical terms inevitable. Second, inclusion gives the opportunity to entice low-level cadres away from the Khmer Rouge and allow the captive population in areas occupied by the

Khmer Rouge some chance to move out of their control. Third, China must have a face-saving way to drop the Khmer Rouge. The theory is that the central government must let the Khmer Rouge demonstrate its incorrigibility beyond any doubt before branding it an outlaw once and for all. China would insist on this political concession before cutting off all aid and permitting the destruction of its protégés.

Much depends on the powers given Sihanouk in his leadership role during the transition and as permanent head of state. Some veteran Sihanouk-watchers charge that the Prince wants only to return to his gilded palace to reign rather than rule and that Hun Sen's game is to entice him into this mainly symbolic role, leaving real power in the KPRP's hands. Sihanouk, however, has stated that he will not return to Cambodia under such conditions, and the thrust of his recent negotiating tactics has been to extract concessions that would strengthen his hand in a settlement. Then there is the question that many veteran Sihanouk-watchers are hesitant to pose out loud—if Sihanouk rules, will he rule well, and for whose benefit ultimately?

How should the United States handle the delicate question of a quadripartite transitional arrangement?

Secretary Baker, in Brunei and repeatedly in Paris, made clear that the United States sees no settlement possible unless the four Cambodian factions can agree among themselves.

If the United States is putting its eggs in Sihanouk's basket, it probably has no option but to accept Sihanouk's and the other Cambodian parties' judgment on including the Khmer Rouge, as distasteful and even dangerous as this may be. At bottom, the modalities must be worked out by the Cambodians themselves, presumably between Sihanouk and Hun Sen—their necks are on the block. If they do, it would be senseless for the United States to reject the bargain, even were it in our power to do so.

There is a more dangerous possibility, however, that if the Khmer Rouge are excluded (or exclude themselves) from a coalition arrangement, Sihanouk might then reject cooperation with Hun Sen and return to an active alliance with the Khmer Rouge and a continuation of the anti-PRK insurgency. This would destroy the current round of Paris negotiations and embark Cambodia on the road to open civil war. ASEAN would be split; Japan, the EC, and Australia might support the PRK (and implicitly Vietnam's position). The NCR would also be badly divided. Under these circumstances the United States could no longer support Sihanouk, even if it chose to do so—anything smacking of aid to the Khmer Rouge would be morally and politically indefensible. Promoting the cause of the noncommunist Cambodians would become nigh impossible. The only option would be to abstain and in effect accept the present Phnom Penh regime as the basis upon which to build a new Cambodia. Ironically, this is where negotiations may lead in any case.

Assuming that the above unhappy scenario does not come to pass, there are measures that the United States can take to obtain terms that give the noncommunists the best possible chances for survival in the context of Sihanouk–Hun Sen cooperation, and it is here that we should be active.

U.S. BILATERAL DIPLOMACY

The single most important U.S. effort must be with China. All U.S. policy decisions with regard to Cambodia, and Vietnam for that matter, since 1979 have been taken with one nervous eye cocked to China's reaction. Granted, our bilateral relationship is currently extremely brittle. We should nonetheless speak bluntly and with a priority not yet attached to our concern for an equitable Cambodia settlement. Any lingering sense of need to placate China on Cambodia should have vanished with the massacre in Tiananmen Square and subsequent repression. Diplomatic approaches to eliminate all assistance to the Khmer Rouge must be renewed. A strong argument can be made that China's broader interests in East Asia would be well served by terminating the connection to Pol Pot and the genocidal Democratic Kampuchea—it is hard to believe that Beijing does not already understand this fact.

Skepticism is widespread about the completeness of the Vietnamese military withdrawal and possible "stay-behinds" in the form of Vietnamese troopers integrated into Cambodian units, Vietnamese settlers, *Khmer krom* (ethnic Cambodians living in the Vietnamese Mekong delta), or other "Cambodians with Vietnamese minds," as the Khmer Rouge describe them. The United States should offer to coordinate its intelligence resources with China, Thailand, and other countries having such capability to determine as accurately as possible the state of affairs on the ground during and after the Vietnamese departure. The United States should explain to China that it intends to use reconstruction assistance in ways which would promote pluralism and diminish chances of domination of Cambodia by pro-Vietnam elements.

Bilateral discussions with Thailand are also critical. U.S.–Thai relations have been disturbed in the past two years because of trade and intellectual property rights disputes and, more recently, Prime Minister Chatichai's opening to Hun Sen. Another issue has already been added to the list of bilateral headaches: freedom of choice for displaced Cambodians who have fled Khmer Rouge control into the ranks of the NCR. The United States is reportedly taking the international lead in urging Thailand to allow these people to move to camps either under international supervision or under the administration of Sihanouk or Son Sann. Some have tried to return to their homes. The Khmer Rouge must be prevented from forcibly moving their captive population into the Cardamom Mountains for use as cannon fodder. Similarly, the United States should press for greater access to Khmer Rouge camps by UNBRO, UNHCR, and the International Committee of the Red Cross (ICRC).[6]

The Soviet Union has no great interest in perpetuating the Cambodia problem beyond concern over Vietnam's security, and it has many reasons to reduce the visibility of the issue. Prolonged conflict in Cambodia is antithetical to the basic thrust of Gorbachev's Asia and Pacific peace offensive and to the image he seeks in Southeast Asia. If the USSR wants a government in Phnom Penh that tilts strongly toward Vietnam, it will have to decide how much it is willing to sacrifice its relations with

91

ASEAN. The United States has engaged in detailed discussions on Cambodia with the Soviets in Paris and elsewhere, and this bilateral channel should continue to be exploited.

Would a communist government, or one identified with the socialist bloc, be essential from the Soviet perspective? Perhaps not. In addition to security for Vietnam, Moscow wants regional stability; tranquil relations between Cambodia and its neighbors would be more easily arranged if ideology were less important. Again, Poland and Hungary come to mind. In *realpolitik* a sound rationale exists for an agreement between China, the Soviet Union, and the United States to work for a solution protecting the interests of Vietnam and Thailand, as well as the majority of Cambodians.

The U.S. message to Vietnam should be clear: Cooperate in a durable pluralist solution and there will be no threat to Vietnam's security; moreover, immediate economic and trade benefits will accrue. If, however, intransigence leads to a single-party state under Hanoi's thumb, violence, instability, and more border trouble are sure to occur. This is not a threat, just a statement of political reality.

Now is the time for Washington and Hanoi to sit down at a senior level to discuss in precise detail why an equitable compromise settlement in Cambodia can contribute to the solution of a number of regional problems, not the least being China's hostility to Vietnam on this particular issue. Vietnam must be convinced that toughing it out for a one-party, unabashedly pro-Vietnam Cambodian state will only bring long-term grief and delay enjoyment of the fruits of its military withdrawal.

This kind of frank conversation on issues well beyond Cambodia—for example, Vietnam's intentions in the region, problems of renovation, the future of the bilateral relationship—is overdue and is surely appropriate at this fluid stage in Southeast Asian affairs.

As for the Phnom Penh regime, if we must accept the Khmer Rouge presence as part of the quadripartite solution—at least in the transition—because they are part of the problem, why should we not do the same for the PRK? ASEAN talks to Hun Sen; the

Thai government wines and dines him in Bangkok and has all but recognized his regime; Sihanouk and Son Sann talk with him for hours. The argument against the United States talking directly to Hun Sen rests on the grounds that this would undermine Sihanouk's negotiating position by implying recognition of the PRK and thereby its "legitimacy."

This reasoning is flawed. In the current fluid situation, such contact would not hurt Sihanouk, if handled correctly, and it actually could strengthen his position by emphasizing engagement in the Cambodia problem. The message to Hun Sen would be simple: the advantages accruing to you and your KPRP partisans from a genuine coalition with the noncommunists would be substantial in terms of controlling the Khmer Rouge, getting reconstruction aid, attracting outside investment, mollifying China, and moving onto ASEAN's economic playing field.

None of this would be news to Hun Sen, who already appreciates the value of diversification in foreign affairs (and no doubt envies Thailand's virtuosity in this regard), but hearing it directly from the United States would carry authority and political impact.

INTERNATIONALIZATION

All parties, internal and external, agree on the need for an internationalization of a Cambodia settlement. The problem already involves many countries directly and is a fixture on the UN General Assembly's calendar year after year. Opinions differ on what form future international involvement should take. Gaining precise agreements on this aspect of a settlement may determine how soon peace comes to Cambodia and how long it lasts. The international conference in Paris, which opened on July 30, 1989, appears to be the key venue for this process.

The status of Cambodia's UN seat will probably have to be changed before an agreement on a major UN role can be reached. The Soviet Union believes that the UN "could play a proper role in the process of a political settlement," and seems to be encouraging one.[7] Vietnam has been opposed because of the

ASEAN-sponsored International Conference on Kampuchea Resolution of 1981, successive annual votes in the General Assembly against Vietnam's occupation, and the fact that the CGDK occupies the UN seat.

The vacant seat formula, in which the DK would have its credentials withdrawn and no successor presented, is one alternative. It leaves the "legitimacy" question moot. Other variations would be to credential the two noncommunist groups and the PRK into tripartite sharing of the seat or to name the State of Cambodia to the seat but let it remain inactive (that is, no delegation present). China's agreement would be needed for any of these options. ASEAN has these and other formulas under consideration for possible use at the right time in negotiations, but until a comprehensive solution is in final draft, credentialing the PRK, as SOC or otherwise, would not be acceptable to either ASEAN or the United States.

The vacant seat formula appears to hold the most promise. If China can be persuaded to accept it, the United Nations as a body could become more active in attaining that settlement, as described below. Since 1982 UN Undersecretary Rafeeudin Ahmed, the secretary general's troubleshooter for the Cambodia problem, has been shuttling quietly between the ASEAN capitals, Hanoi, Phnom Penh, Beijing, and Moscow to gather a sense of where each of the parties stands on a future role for the UN. He was present at JIM 1 and JIM 2, and has visited with all the Cambodian parties regularly. His position as a representative of the secretary general's office rather than as an emissary of the United Nations itself has made him an acceptable negotiator.

For the United Nations to move beyond this "good offices" function and assume major responsibility for observing and controlling the peace process, unanimous agreement among the parties is essential. The UN will refuse to involve itself in a major fashion if the parties, internal and external, cannot agree first on the overall parameters of a compromise settlement. This agreement could come at the Paris international conference or through the UN Security Council, and the secretary general's office could be helpful behind the scenes. But unless there is genuine political will to resolve the problem step by step and an agreement to stop shooting, then the UN as an organization, with Lebanon in mind, will certainly not become involved.

The United Nations can best perform this coordinating and implementing function, and it should be included from the beginning—that is, in supervising and verifying the actual withdrawal of the PAVN from Cambodian soil. Its effectiveness in this role would set the tone for the success or failure of the subsequent peacekeeping continuum. In light of the annual UN votes on Cambodia, however, and the continued assignment of the UN seat to the CGDK, some trade-off regarding the status of Cambodia's UN seat (three- or four-party sharing, or the vacant-seat formula) will probably have to take place to give the PRK and Vietnam enough "face" to go along with a more comprehensive UN role in observation.

The United Nations does not wish to become involved in the supervision of the withdrawal unless it is part of a comprehensive settlement agreement to which the Cambodian parties have committed themselves ahead of time and which the UN Security Council is inclined to accept as a valid process.[8] This fact has spurred on consideration of the UN role and has made the nature and timing of the PAVN's withdrawal, which in fact kicks off the transition to a new government, critically important.

Vietnam would prefer to conduct the withdrawal on its own terms and for maximum advantage, and in order to protect the image of "sovereignty" of the SOC (or PRK) from whose territory and under whose aegis the Vietnamese volunteers are leaving. Yet, Hanoi must have international approbation. If the withdrawal has no credible verification, Beijing will deny its validity and continue to support Pol Pot. In all likelihood, China will use whatever justification it can find to deny that Vietnam has completely withdrawn.

Consequently, an international control mechanism (ICM) must be established. The PAVN's withdrawal will in effect become part of the settlement even in the absence of a comprehensive settlement agreement. The choices of an observation process could establish the pattern for next steps in the transition. It is consequently critical to have an ICM formally involved from the beginning to observe and verify the PAVN withdrawal. Objectively, it would seem that Vietnam would be ill-advised to stonewall ASEAN, China, and the rest of the world on this issue. The dispatch of a United Nations–led mission to evaluate the situation in Cambodia as a result of an earlier agreement at the Paris conference is an encouraging but tentative indicator.

Several warnings must be sounded here.

First, a role of peacekeeping by force of arms for the UN ICM in Cambodia had been ruled out by most observers for obvious practical reasons. The country's size, terrain, and the vicious animosities among the antagonists make it inconceivable that the Blue Helmets could keep the warring parties apart if the political will for reconciliation was not present as a result of a comprehensive agreement.

Second, the ICM's function would not be a multinational counterinsurgency. That job will have to be done ultimately by the Cambodians themselves. Nonetheless, the ICM would be sufficiently armed for self-protection and made up of highly trained, mobile combat personnel quickly adaptable to hardy rural surroundings. It might number as many as 4,000 or more men (versus the 600 observers initially suggested by Vietnam for the ICC; Sihanouk wants 10,000), which is about the strength of the UN Namibia force. It would be under the direct command of a UN general, who in turn would report to the secretary general. Its units would be scattered throughout the country but with maximum placement in western, northwestern, and southwestern areas where the Khmer Rouge are most active. All this, however, might take months to put in place.

Third, an ICM would be hideously expensive. Four thousand men with their support apparatus would cost many hundreds of millions of dollars per year. Japan may pay part but not all. Who will pay the rest?

The Cambodian parties will have to settle the central question of what becomes of their standing armies. The CGDK has proposed four armies of 10,000 men each; the PRK rejected this plan out of hand, since it would be outnumbered three to one.

The Khmer Rouge are not about to disband any of their elite units; they may be put into civilian-appearing groups but they will still be Khmer Rouge fighters. The PRK is not oblivious to this, and it too will probably not stand down any of its better troops. What becomes of the PRK's civil militia, or village guards, who have been well armed, is another sticky question to be thrashed out. Sihanouk has consistently charged that these militia, plus Vietnamese stay-behinds, would prevent Cambodia from ever becoming truly independent.[9]

The election campaign period could last up to a year; it would take months for the noncommunists to get organized in the countryside. The ICM would help monitor the campaign process and the setting up of polling places. Additional international observers would be needed at voting time. The entire process of organizing "free, fair, and open" elections is extraordinarily complex and expensive. Finally, who will guarantee rural security against violations by the Khmer Rouge or coercion by other factions?

With so many issues to be resolved in designing and implementing a comprehensive settlement, it is perhaps enough to say that the United States should be involved directly at every stage of the negotiations in the effort to make the final agreement work. The United States should not be expected to contribute to the ICM military force in Cambodia, but American civilians could take part in specialist functions. For example, we have extensive experience in election procedures and should be able to contribute to that process with people and hardware, if that is needed.

U.S. SUPPORT FOR THE NONCOMMUNISTS IN AN INTERNATIONALIZED CONTEXT

The public emphasis on lethal aid—let us call it guns, ammunition, rockets, hand grenades, and other things that kill—has distracted attention from the essence of the noncommunists' predicament in the current fluid environment. While more material assistance, including guns and more money, would improve Sihanouk's bargaining position somewhat, what will be decisive in military and political matters are the noncommunists' leadership, motivation, organization, dedication, and discipline. These qualities take years to develop and cannot be supplied by foreigners.

Aid under the Solarz program has been helpful because it began in 1985 and concentrated on preparing the Cambodians in refugee camps to run their own affairs, if and when peace comes to Cambodia and they are allowed to return home. But the program has been small compared to the need. Sihanouk and Son Sann are far from achieving a critical mass in the realm of political and administrative organization, and time is very short. Regrettably, years have been wasted because the NCR has not been able to focus in a disciplined fashion on its future political objectives. The emphasis has been on forcing Vietnam to withdraw—and that does not constitute a viable political platform in a coalition government.

Until now, the noncommunists' only credible military asset has been its unholy alliance with the Khmer Rouge—a deadly two-edged sword. It remains to be seen if a rapid infusion of M-16s and mortars can make the ANS and KPNLF more "effective," whatever that term means in the current negotiating context. The Khmer Rouge menace is not going to be countered simply by giving more arms to the NCR. The proponents of such aid are talking in terms of "survival;" beyond that the military mission is vague. Only by China and Thailand cutting off Pol Pot's lifelines and removing the hard-core leaders can the military threat from the Khmer Rouge be contained.

Sihanouk's assets are political: his charisma with Cambodians, his support in the international community, his association with China, *and* the fact that Hun Sen needs him. One of the Prince's political advantages, Vietnam's ten-year status as an aggressive occupying power, will be gone. If there is no settlement, the State of Cambodia will become the enemy. The Phnom Penh regime's steady economic progress and adept public relations campaign changes the chemistry of the struggle. The contest with the KPRP will be fought as much on political and economic as on military grounds, and if Sihanouk and the non-communists remain guerrillas bent on disruption, they would not be heroes to the Cambodian peasantry. It is obvious that the noncommunists must have the means to defend themselves against the Khmer Rouge, but large quantities of arms at this late date will not redress their basic organizational and leadership weaknesses during the next stage of the Cambodia problem.

We return to the question, what does the United States want out of a settlement—simply no return to power of the Khmer Rouge, or no return *plus* a pluralist society that would be comfortable for our noncommunist friends? If the answer is the latter, the United States should accept the ramifications of that commitment and be prepared to provide more material support to FUNCINPEC and the KPNLF in the negotiating period, and then political and moral support during transition and after a settlement. If pluralism is to have any chance of survival, the United States must commit itself not for one or two fiscal years but over the long haul. The commitment should be a carefully measured one so that our noncommunist friends are not led to believe that the Marines will come to their rescue or that we will fund them in something like Nicaraguan Contra status. The Cambodians must take primary responsibility themselves.

Reconstruction aid must be integrated with the programs of the international community, and it should begin as early as possible in the transition period, before elections for a permanent government are held. To the greatest extent feasible, it should be given to all Cambodian civilians regardless of political persuasion, and portrayed up front as nonpartisan. Obviously, no aid of any sort should be given to or through the existing Khmer Rouge apparatus. The United States should encourage and facilitate the activities of voluntary agencies and nongovernment organizations, many of which are already active in Cambodia, to expand their work and to get out into the countryside.

All this would be a statement on behalf of a new Cambodian society seeking genuine reconciliation among formerly opposed factions. To work, the American aid component must be nonthreatening; we should make sure Vietnam and the KPRP understand our objectives yet advise them frankly against trying to undermine other groups engaging in legitimate political activity. Perhaps most important, the U.S. effort would be one part of an international effort—we are not going it alone this time.

This proposal is a tall order for an American policy heretofore only marginally involved in a Cambodia settlement. The job will be made even more difficult because the U.S. government is poorly informed about Cambodian society and the state of affairs in Cambodia today.

The key to a successful coalition of the FUNCINPEC, the KPNLF, and the KPRP lies less in Sihanouk and Son Sann's strength than in Hun Sen and the KPRP's weakness. The latter need support against the Khmer Rouge and cooperation in the reconstruction effort. As noted previously, there is already a degree of quiet cooperation in the field between military units of the NCR and the PRK army. This cooperation must be replicated in the economic sector and expanded manyfold in order to guarantee the noncommunists' survivability—and Cambodia's stability and prosperity.

PRK officials have professed the regime's desire to let many flowers bloom. They emphasize the pragmatic, as opposed to the ideological, nature of the top leadership, its Khmerness and intention to protect Cambodia through diverse relationships rather than reliance on Vietnam. They also say Sihanouk and Son Sann's people could make valuable contributions if reconciliation becomes a fact.

Perhaps. It depends on the terms. The PRK's economic pragmatism and enthusiasm for the private sector are impressive, but to this date the KPRP in its public pronouncements and in the new constitution of the "State of Cambodia" shows that it is still reluctant to share political power inside Cambodia in any meaningful fashion. Yet Hun Sen requires the substance as well as the form of reconciliation, and he needs the active involvement of noncommunist Cambodians in and outside the country in order to gain international acceptance and economic aid from the nonsocialist world. Thus there is reciprocal need. The question is, will the KPRP pay the price of surrendering its monopoly on political control? Again, this was one of the key issues being debated in Paris and it remains unresolved.

The economic potential of the noncommunists is their ace in the hole during current negotiations and for the future. Individuals in the overseas Khmer communities have already demonstrated considerable interest in returning as investors or as businessmen. Under conditions of peace and with reasonable guarantees—of personal security as well as investment—the trickle of interest could become a flood. Cambodia's tourist potential is extensive. In terms of soil and water resources, its agricultural sector could become among the most productive in Southeast Asia. What counts even more than individual private investment is the sense of respectability and legitimacy that the noncommunist participation would lend to the coalition regime. These qualities are essential to attract the international banks and corporations. Also important are the expatriates' business expertise, contacts in the Western world, and technical skills—all in desperately short supply in Cambodia today.

Democracy, or pluralism, if one wishes to call it that, seems incongruous in the context of Cambodia's barbaric experiences over recent decades. Historically, such a concept has never been part of Cambodian political experience. Yet strange forces are stirring in U.S. relations with the Marxist-Leninist world—witness the thrust of American policy in Eastern Europe and the opening up of Poland and Hungary, not to mention the Soviet Union. If the United States finds it politically useful to extend a helping hand to countries it not long ago called "Soviet satellites," it should also find it possible to work with a coalition organized by Sihanouk, Son Sann, and their communist Cambodian brethren, even though the latter (excluding the Khmer Rouge apparatus) may be in a dominant role. The best way to make a commitment to Sihanouk and Son Sann effective is to persuade the Vietnamese and the KPRP that the stability and economic reconstruction they so ardently want will be attainable only through a political solution that allows noncommunist Cambodians not only to survive but to take part fully in governance and to prosper.

It remains to be seen if the noncommunists' assets can be parlayed into political leverage and firm guarantees of a pluralist political process. One thing seems certain: If the new system is to work, it will have to be more Khmer than communist.

8

THE STRANGE COLD WARMTH OF NORMALIZATION

Can the United States advance its strategic interests in East Asia by normalizing relations with the Socialist Republic of Vietnam? The answer is clearly yes—in the context of an acceptable settlement in Cambodia.[1]

As noted in the preceding chapters, all signs point to a Vietnamese withdrawal, if not in September then soon thereafter. The political environment for a comprehensive Cambodia settlement, however, has not yet been established. The disquieting possibility remains that no settlement, either partial or comprehensive, will be reached during the current negotiations. In that case, Cambodia could well descend once more into chaos. If Vietnamese intransigence was the cause, then all bets on normalization would be off. Yet intractability on the part of Sihanouk and China could be equally responsible for a failure of negotiations toward a comprehensive settlement. This would place the United States in a quandary of how to proceed with Vietnam in the light of continued impasse in Cambodia. It points up a basic dilemma of U.S. policy which is held hostage to an unreliable Sihanouk and to a China whose regional objectives are not necessarily compatible with ours.

Historically, there is no small irony here. In the early 1970s, Cambodia as a nation was secondary (in truth, all but discardable) to the overriding requirement of ending America's massive involvement in Vietnam. Now it is Cambodia, or, more accurately, Vietnam's performance in Cambodia, that determines what happens between our two countries. Vietnam *as Vietnam* has ceased being a factor of much importance in the East Asia and Pacific calculations of the United States.

In a new and probably expanded U.S.–Vietnam relationship, which may get under way in the relatively near future, the

United States should devise a policy framework that extends for more than one fiscal year and that addresses bilateral issues well beyond the current array of humanitarian concerns.

Once we go through that doorway of establishing diplomatic relations, what do we want from the relationship?

The United States wants continued Vietnamese support for an equitable Cambodia political settlement that, with regard to the noncommunist Cambodian factions of Sihanouk and Son Sann, Vietnam and the Cambodian communists will respect. Obviously the Khmer Rouge must be prevented from returning to power, and this is a common interest. The United States also wants continued progress on bilateral humanitarian issues already on the table with Vietnam. Over the longer term, it wants to see an end to Vietnamese expansionism, less Vietnamese reliance on the Soviet Union, and an evolution of a Vietnamese economy that is increasingly linked to ASEAN and the world's free market system.

On a different level, the United States should hope for, and do what it appropriately can to promote, internal changes in Vietnam leading to greater freedom for the Vietnamese people and a degree of political openness in their society.

These are ambitious, perhaps idealistic, goals. They raise tough practical questions about what can be realistically achieved.

On Cambodia, knowing how badly Vietnam wants the fruits of normalization, should the United States withhold the actual opening of relations until Vietnam has proved its adherence to the terms of a settlement? Is normalization divisible, that is, should we normalize diplomatic relations but keep the trade embargo in place as a hedge against Vietnamese performance? Or should we perhaps maintain our "hold" on loans from international financial institutions in order to obtain Vietnamese concessions? Would "interests sections" be a useful first step as an alternative to embassies?

In the longer term, to what extent should concern for human rights influence U.S. policy toward Vietnam, and how can we make our influence felt? What economic and humanitarian assistance should the United States consider in the context of a future relationship?

In strategic matters, a number of issues are worth contemplating even though they do not bear immediately upon the normalization process. What are Vietnam's "legitimate security interests" in the context of some sort of "special relationship" with Laos and Cambodia? How can the United States reduce Vietnam's dependence on the Soviet Union?

NORMALIZATION—FICTION AND REALITY

Normalization, strictly defined, refers to the establishment of diplomatic relations: the exchange of ambassadors, the granting of exequaturs to consuls, and then everything that flows from this in terms of travel, commerce, communications, and diplomatic intercourse. Normal relations are ruptured when states disagree so violently that they no longer wish to treat with each other; or they are withheld by one state to demonstrate disapproval of another and to force it to change its conduct. The latter applies to the U.S. policy toward Vietnam.

There are gradations short of "fully normalized" relations, for example where chargés d'affaires instead of ambassadors are present, the case with Laos and the United States since 1975. There is the aberrational format of "interests sections" in an embassy of a third country (the United States in the Swiss embassy in Havana) when nations wish to do business without implying approval. The ploy of "liaison offices" was used between the United States and the People's Republic of China from 1973 to 1979, until the question of breaking diplomatic and military ties with the Republic of China (Taiwan) was resolved.

Lawyers say that diplomatic recognition and its consequence, diplomatic relations, need not connote approval. With regard to Vietnam, this textbook interpretation is irrelevant. Like it or not, an immense amount of political and emotional baggage has been piled on normalization because it has come to symbolize an end to a tragic war and the opening of a new era.

The quality of "forgive and forget" has been unacceptable to a number of Americans.

Normalization is not some magical act achieved by the stroke of a pen. Since the United States has never had normal relations with Vietnam or the Vietnamese, either North or South, it should not expect to develop such a relationship quickly or easily. The initial step, establishing diplomatic relations and opening embassies, can be straightforward once the political decision has been taken. Many of the administrative procedures were formulated in 1977–78. What comes after is a different matter. The really difficult problems in the relationship will begin when the Socialist Republic of Vietnam opens up the former Republic of Vietnam chancery on Sheridan Circle in northwest Washington, closed April 30, 1975, and the United States reoccupies the faded green villa on Ly Thuong Kiet street in Hanoi, which it left in July 1954 after the Geneva Conference.

The process will take a lot of hard work by both sides on specific issues. Improvement of official relations will be governed by cold calculations of political, economic, and strategic advantage. For example, at the outset there will be tough negotiations on claims by private U.S. companies against the SRV that total more than $99 million, not including interest accrued since 1975. The United States holds more than $150 million in frozen Vietnamese assets. Despite some favorable factors noted above, official mutual mistrust will make the road of diplomatic intercourse rocky. The United States cannot ignore Hanoi's past negotiating style or its record in reneging on agreements. Some pro-Vietnam activist groups in the United States are under the impression that sweetness and light will prevail once the nirvana of normalization is reached. This attitude is misleading and harmful to the long-range objective of building a sound bilateral relationship. "Healing the wounds of war" and "putting the past behind us" are noble sentiments but insufficient grounds on which to build durable understanding and mutual trust.

The Vietnamese government retains many of its wartime fixations and repressive practices, but the United States will have to deal with them just as it deals with those of the Soviet Union,

China, and other governments with policies we do not approve. As the American public and the administration take a fresh look at Vietnam, it would be wise to bear in mind that whatever we think of the Hanoi regime and its conduct before and after 1975, the Vietnamese people are not our enemies—they never have been.

This perspective may outrage some Americans; hatred, anger, and frustration are the residue of war. Among many other Americans, however, there is compassion for the Vietnamese as individuals, an appreciation of their culture, and even a conviction that not everything Americans did in Vietnam was dirty or deplorable. Americans should differentiate between the government of the SRV and the Vietnamese Communist Party, on the one hand, and the people of the country of Vietnam, on the other. This, of course, applies to our dealings with all totalitarian states—but it is particularly relevant to our future relations with Vietnam.

In fact, a unique relationship with Vietnam already exists as a consequence of our long and intimate association with the South. In the North, despite past hostilities, Americans today are often greeted with warmth and openness. Any visitor to Vietnam in 1989 senses the bittersweet inheritance from the vast American involvement and the more than two million Americans who served "in-country." The fact that more than three-quarters of a million Americans of Vietnamese descent now live in the United States creates an eerie, ambivalent intimacy. Over the next decades the United States and Vietnam should have the capacity to construct a people-to-people relationship that will have geopolitical, economic, and psychological value on both sides.

The war-generation leaders are finally beginning to pass from the Politburo. No doubt the younger leaders are as tough as Truong Chinh and Le Duan (both dead) and Pham Van Dong and Le Duc Tho (both alive but failing). The new leaders may well harbor the same ambitions for dominance in Indochina. But they will have slept with the Russians and tasted traditional pressures from the People's Republic of China. There will be pressures from other quarters. As students in Eastern Europe they will have observed political ferment and economic liberalization in Marxist societies. Unlike their fathers, they will visit Bangkok, Jakarta, and, eventually, Taipei and Seoul to see what non-Marxist economic development is all about. Some of their children will, it is to be hoped, study in the United States. For stark reasons of national security the new leaders must diversify Vietnam's external relations.

The failure of Marxism-Leninism as an economic philosophy is evident even to the hard-liners in Hanoi. An awkward overhauling has been under way for several years to make dogma and practice fit contemporary conditions. Some leaders are looking at models in ASEAN and the newly industrialized economies of Asia. They are also observing, no doubt with some anxiety, the convulsions of protest and demands for change elsewhere in the communist world.

Events with profound implications for Vietnam have taken place in China. It is impossible to predict the eventual impact of the popular uprising in China, and the manner in which it was crushed, upon the Lesser Dragon to the South. The basic forces at work in China are also present in Vietnam and will sooner or later seek expression. The Vietnamese people are intelligent, contentious, and vigorous. Their aspirations for a better life are not much different from those of other cultures. Ho Chi Minh's favorite aphorism, "Nothing is more precious than independence and freedom" was originally applied to French colonial rule, and later to the war with the United States. One sees and hears it often these days in Vietnam—it bears an especially sardonic meaning for the Vietnamese people.

The Vietnamese Communist Party is determined, as are its counterparts in the Soviet Union and China, to retain political control. Although no outsider can predict how much or how fast change will occur, Vietnamese communism will have to adjust to the political and economic forces already beginning to challenge the essence of the party's power well before the spring 1989 events in China.

Vietnam needs the United States. If we take the trouble to understand Vietnam's history, the changes taking place in the communist party, and the incipient discontent in Vietnamese society, and above all if we negotiate patiently and play for the long haul while the old order changes, valuable opportunities—in political as well as human terms—should emerge from the bilateral relationship.

HUMANITARIAN ISSUES—THE CUTTING EDGE OF NORMALIZATION

POW/MIAs, the Orderly Departure Program, Amerasians, and emigration for "reeducation inmates" make up the substance of the abnormal bilateral U.S. agenda with Vietnam since 1975. The venues for discussions have included Hanoi, Geneva, Honolulu, Bangkok, New York, Ho Chi Minh City, and (in the case of MIA searches) some rather remote parts of the Vietnamese countryside. As normalization unfolds, these particular humanitarian issues will continue to set the tone of the new bilateral relationship.

The missing-in-action question remains an important adjunct to the normalization process. The Bush administration is confident that the Vietnamese ". . . understand that the pace and scope of our relations would depend on continued progress on the POW/MIA issue. . . . While this is a humanitarian issue which should be pursued separately on its merits, progress in this area must continue if there is to be political support in this country for a fully normalized relationship."[2]

The appointment in mid-1987 of retired General John W. Vessey, Jr., former chairman of the Joint Chiefs of Staff, as Special Presidential Emissary for Humanitarian Affairs marked the beginning of a new phase on what is still the most neuralgic bilateral humanitarian issue, Americans missing in Southeast Asia. General Vessey visited the SRV in August 1987 and obtained Hanoi's commitment to accelerate efforts to help find MIA remains and provide information. In return, and for the first time, the United States agreed to look into certain humanitarian concerns of the Vietnamese as a result of the war. The nature of the dialogue was thereby changed. Since then, Vessey (who was reappointed to his position by President Bush) has been the senior point of contact with the Vietnamese.[3]

Results point to a decision by Vietnam to do what is necessary to satisfy the United States on POW/MIAs. In an unprecedented display of cooperation, Hanoi accepted a standing U.S. offer to conduct joint, U.S.–funded searches in provincial locations believed to have MIA remains. Using American jeeps, excavation machinery, computers, and a variety of specialized equipment, five joint search operations have taken place in North Vietnamese provinces since September 1988. As of July 31, 1989, 231 sets of remains had been recovered; 64 of these were positively identified as missing U.S. servicemen. The SRV has cooperated well, providing in addition numerous bits of information relevant to the fate of MIAs. Rice farmers have witnessed the strange spectacle of U.S. vehicles and personnel roaming the North Vietnamese countryside with their government counterparts in a way that would have been considered unthinkable a few years ago.

In late 1987, under the auspices of the Vessey mission, the first of three U.S. prosthetics teams visited Vietnam to survey problems of the disabled. A flow of prosthetic devices began then and continues to this date. In February 1989, "Operation Smile," a private philanthropic medical organization based in Norfolk, Virginia, conducted an eight-day surgical visit to Hanoi during which U.S. doctors performed cleft palate and burn scar reconstruction operations on 103 Vietnamese children. The American team established links with the SRV Ministry of Health and hospital staffs that will be used for similar medical visits in the future. Operation Smile had the good offices and logistical support of the U.S. Departments of State and Defense, including airlift of supplies and personnel, and was arranged through cooperation of various Vietnamese government agencies and the Hanoi Viet Duc Hospital. It generated enormous good will in Vietnam and represents a useful pattern for future reciprocal humanitarian cooperation.*

* The American Friends Service Committee and the Mennonite Central Committee have carried on private prosthetics and other medical assistance programs in Vietnam since the war with the permission of the U.S. government.

The U.S. humanitarian commitment under the Vessey initiative was a gesture calculated to stimulate Vietnamese cooperation on POW/MIAs, a sweetener the United States had not chosen to offer previously in such precise terms. Foreign Minister Thach wanted a weightier American contribution to satisfy his own political needs but finally agreed to the deal. It might not have been accepted had Thach not known that Cambodia was entering the end game and that the military occupation was to be terminated in the fairly near future. Why give the United States what it wanted in humanitarian matters (MIA cooperation) until removal of the political barrier to normalization (Cambodia) was in sight? POW/MIA cooperation has waxed and waned for more than a decade according to the temperature of the political water of the moment. But in 1987 the Politburo found good reasons to respond positively to Vessey's clear signal. The Vietnamese logic in all this is instructive.

Of the 2,347 Americans still in MIA status as of July 1989, all but one (for symbolic purposes) are now listed by the Pentagon as "Killed in action, body not recovered." Nevertheless, many Americans are nagged by the possibility that live American servicemen may yet be held prisoner in Southeast Asia. One of the keys to resolving the issue is accounting for the "discrepancy cases," those cases where an individual is believed to have survived his incident (such as bailing out of an aircraft and being seen later on the ground) and to have come into the hands of Vietnamese forces. In these discrepancy cases, the serviceman did not return with other former POWs in 1973; his body has not been returned, and no explanation of his fate has been provided. General Vessey has given the Vietnamese information on 252 such cases, of which 70 were categorized as "most compelling." As of May 1989, 13 of the 70 and 28 of the larger group of 252 have been resolved through the recovery or return of identified remains.[4]

At some point, the administration will have to decide when a satisfactory resolution of this sensitive matter has been achieved and tell the American people honestly what more can reasonably be expected.

As for Amerasians, by summer 1989 about 7,000 Viet-namese of American parentage had left Vietnam for a new life in the United States. The majority of these Amerasians, who were already in their teens, were accompanied by Vietnamese mothers or close relatives (13,000 additional persons) for a total of 20,000 emigrants; only a small percentage were united with their American fathers after arriving. An estimated 7,000 Am-erasians and their close family (another 23,000) remain in Viet-nam; a certain number of these are believed to be content in their present circumstances and may not wish to leave. The Amera-sian program, after a difficult beginning, has worked quite well since 1982.

The Orderly Departure Program, which in fiscal year 1988 moved 12,230 Vietnamese to the United States, in addition to 6,838 to France, Canada, and elsewhere, presents more difficult problems. Its rationale is to give Vietnamese who worked with the U.S. government or were associated with the former Saigon regime—most of whom now suffer discrimination in Vietnam—the opportunity to move to the United States as refugees. About 19,500 are expected to move in fiscal year 1989 under the U.S. refugee quota. As many as 5,000 additional persons will depart during 1989 for the United States with regular immigrant visas.[5]

The situation of former inmates of "reeducation camps" who seek to leave their country is especially poignant. About 11,000 such persons, most of whom held the rank of major and above in the army or an equivalent status in the police or civil bureaucracy of the former government, have declared their desire to emigrate. With immediate family members, they would number between 50,000 and 60,000. Some spent ten years or more under harsh conditions, and on being freed are barred from any but menial employment. Their children have limited educational opportunities, and other restrictions are attached to their families. These former inmates are likely to be third-class citizens for the rest of their lives.

In principle, the United States should accept for immigra-tion any Vietnamese who is stigmatized by his previous associa-tion with the American presence. In 1984, President Reagan pledged to accept all reeducation camp inmates and their families. Foreign Minister Thach agreed in principle to permit this but subsequently backed out for reasons that are not entirely clear.*

An immigration procedure that uses former rank and reeducation camp inmate status as prime criteria for coming to the United States is potentially inequitable. What about the sergeant or rural development cadre (a sensitive U.S. program for many years) or village official under the Thieu regime who had only a few weeks reeducation but who is nonetheless permanently barred from gainful employment and whose children must suffer for their father's previous role? What about the South Vietnamese soldier who lost his legs in the war and has been refused any sort of help from the government because he served the "puppet regime"? The streets of Ho Chi Minh City and Danang and the ferry boats plying the rivers of the Mekong delta are filled with beggars who once fought for the South or worked at the lowest level (where the suffering was greatest) and consequently did not merit long stays in a prison. During the war, they only saw Americans flying by in helicopters and certainly never talked with them. While many have been able to integrate themselves into the new society, the plight of others is probably as dire as that of the colonels and politicians who landed in reeducation camp and whom the United States is committed to help.† There are no accurate figures on how many Vietnamese might fall into this category.

The absence of progress between August 1988 and July 1989 in arranging emigration by former reeducation camp in-

* Top communist party cadres reportedly harbor intense hatred for their former foes despite the enfeebled state of most of the latter after years of "reeducation." In July 1988, Thach and the Foreign Ministry may have gotten out in front of the Interior Ministry on this issue and were subsequently reined in.

† When it appeared that Hanoi might let former camp inmates leave (per Thach's promise), there was a run on luggage stores in Ho Chi Minh City. Reportedly some former officials who had evaded reeducation camp through bribes or false personal histories were distraught over their poor judgment in 1975, since they would be ineligible for a ticket to the United States.

mates is attributable in part to Hanoi's demand that the U.S. government guarantee that Vietnamese-Americans (specifically former inmates), if permitted to go to the United States, not threaten the SRV's security.[6] The United States can enforce laws that might be applicable to armed incursions into Vietnam from U.S. territory, and it can assure Hanoi that U.S. policy does not condone such activity from any source. But obviously no administration is going to abridge the rights of free speech, advocacy, and assembly, or other constitutional rights of American citizens. The Vietnamese have been bluntly informed to this effect.

VIETNAMESE-AMERICANS AND NORMALIZATION

More than 1.7 million Vietnamese now live outside their country in the West. Another 250,000 have fled to China since 1975. About 750,000 live in the United States, with most of the remainder in France and Canada. Their adjustment generally has been excellent. Vietnamese workers have acquired a reputation for dedication, an ability to learn quickly, and a high innate intelligence. Vietnamese students tend to rank at or near the top of their secondary-school and college classes.

The Vietnamese-American community already wields influence in the politics of certain localities. The National Congress of Vietnamese in America meets regularly to coordinate positions on issues of special interest to the refugee community. It is not inconceivable that southern California's Orange County will elect an American of Vietnamese ancestry to the House of Representatives in a few years and perhaps sooner to local office. Vietnamese-language newspapers have sprung up throughout California and in the greater Washington, D.C., area, and elsewhere around the country.

The community's attitude toward imminent normalization and the dimensions of a new relationship with the home country is split, according to the judgment of Vietnamese-American leaders in touch with sentiment in the various parts of the United States. Very few approve of the Hanoi regime; hatred and contempt is the prevailing sentiment. Yet when it comes to the

114

practicalities of dealing with the regime, attitudes are confused and conflicted. Most Vietnamese-Americans, being political realists, seem to accept the inevitability of normalized diplomatic relations in the near future. Some are even preparing to do business, as indicated by the numerous "Viet kieu" (overseas Vietnamese) circulating in Ho Chi Minh City as guests of the Chamber of Commerce.

A profound sense of loss characterizes Vietnamese living in the United States. Virtually all have relatives and friends still in Vietnam, and a sense of uneasiness about their own prosperity and opportunities compared with the poverty and deprivation of their countrymen is part of the Vietnamese psyche in America. A fair number of the lucky ones here would probably admit that since the United States is not going to try to overthrow the Hanoi government, normalization is the only avenue for improving the lot of their mother country.

A minority of Vietnamese-Americans advocate minimal dealings with the Hanoi regime and would like indefinite political ostracism and economic isolation with the hope of forcing the regime to its knees. Some believe a popular upheaval in Vietnam, and even the disintegration of the communist party, is possible. This vocal minority would include members of the nationalist parties formerly active in Vietnam and persons who served in reeducation camps and escaped by boat or emigrated under the ODP more recently. The latter, having suffered under the communists after "liberation," have prestige; they cannot be easily challenged by those who fled in April 1975 and are now well established in American society. The SRV is keenly aware of the "revanchists" and attacks them in the media.

The community is currently engaged in an internal debate on how best to face the prospect of normalized relations. Boycotts and incidents of violence have been perpetrated against individuals or newspapers speaking in favor of normalization.[7] More responsible persons realize that the SRV, once its embassy opens in Washington, will take advantage of divisions among the expatriates, and believe that they must therefore try to speak with one voice. While in a democracy there are many discordant voices (and Vietnamese are by nature argumentative), responsible community leaders want a consensus on controversial policy issues in the future in order to maintain a common front.

The attitudes of the Vietnamese-American community will not determine the pace of normalization. But they will help shape the administration's thinking on specific aspects of our bilateral relations, notably human rights and provision of financial support to families still in Vietnam. After normalization, such issues are likely to become a source of even greater friction. In the long run, contact with the overseas Vietnamese communities, particularly in America, will be a significant external influence in the evolution of Vietnamese society at home.

NEGOTIATING NORMALIZATION

Some U.S. politicians and public groups may demand preconditions, beyond what has been said on Cambodia, on a variety of issues before establishment of diplomatic relations with Vietnam and before lifting the embargo. In the author's view, it would be unwise to present Hanoi with a laundry list of "demands" or new preconditions.

Once the political decision has been made, negotiations could last a week, or they could last several months. During this process, clear understandings on continued Vietnamese cooperation on the four humanitarian issues (POW/MIA, ODP, Amerasians, reeducation camp inmates) should be established as reasonable elements of a healthy and positive new relationship. The negotiations that set the terms of "fully normalized relations" should include specific provisions for continued Vietnamese cooperation on POW/MIAs: joint searches, access to records that could determine the fate of the missing, and access to locations where Americans have been reported seen alive. In return, the Vietnamese should be able to expect continued, and probably expanded, programs of private and government-facilitated medical and other humanitarian assistance. Judging by Hanoi's actions over the past year, it is reasonable to assume that "unlinked" progress on POW/MIAs will continue to move on its own track.

The children of American fathers from the war era have a special claim, not the least of which is entitlement to American citizenship. From the SRV's political perspective, there would seem to be no reason why those Amerasians who want to come to the United States after normalization should not be allowed to do so. The United States should expect, and make explicit in pre-normalization negotiations, that this would be the case.

In the course of negotiating normalization of relations, the United States should reach an unambiguous agreement with Hanoi on exit permits for former reeducation camp inmates and other individuals of special concern. In negotiations conducted in late July 1989, such an agreement was tentatively concluded.

The practical question is, how much leverage can be feasibly applied to obtain guarantees on issues other than Cambodia and POW/MIAs? The administration will have to study these and related questions carefully. Certain observations on this process would seem in order.

Diplomatic representation should be established at the embassy level with ambassadors present. There is no sensible half-way point. An "interests section," chargé d'affaires status, or liaison office arrangements would inhibit the kind of full and authoritative exchanges that it is to our benefit to have with the Vietnamese.

Interests sections in Hanoi and Washington were proposed in the Congress in mid-1988 as a way of tackling humanitarian issues in the absence of a Cambodia settlement; the proposal was resisted by the Reagan administration and eventually dropped by the Congress. This idea makes even less sense now. Negotiations determining the future of Cambodia, and in reality the direction of Indochina, are underway with the participation of all the major players in the region. Except for emigration of reeducation camp inmates, bilateral humanitarian issues are moving ahead satisfactorily. That was not the case in mid-1988.

Whatever value the interests sections option may have had in the past has been overtaken by events.

Looking beyond our current concerns, the United States should inform the SRV that human rights considerations will be central, not peripheral, in the conduct of bilateral relations. These include our support for a freer flow of information into Vietnam, relaxation of emigration controls and travel generally, greater respect for the civil rights of ethnic minorities, and an amelioration of the status of those in the South still suffering discrimination because of the war. Moreover, the United States should take a strong position on freedom of religion in Vietnam—the practice of Buddhism and Christianity, and unfettered operation of religious institutions. The latter should be permitted to receive private financial contributions from the United States in pursuit of traditional functions such as education and social welfare. Chaplains, monks, and other clerics who were imprisoned for their beliefs should be released and their rights restored. Before normalization occurs the SRV should be left in no doubt that the regime's human rights performance will significantly affect the future course of relations.

Some observers have proposed that the United States maintain all or part of existing trade and investment restrictions until Vietnam complies with U.S. requirements on a variety of issues, notably Cambodia and human rights observance. Concerning the former, full implementation of a Cambodia settlement and continued adherence to its terms by Vietnam is and must continue to be an international concern. If sanctions were to be reapplied, this would have to be done multilaterally, in which case the United States would have to work with ASEAN, Japan, and others to bring appropriate pressure to bear.

Once a satisfactory settlement is reached, however, it would be all but impossible to perpetuate U.S. sanctions against the policies of friends and allies on economic and trade relations. The United States could, however, use its influence in the Asian Development Bank and other international financial institutions as leverage on specific issues of concern, as it has in the past. But the initial position for purposes of normalization should be as previously stated: "In the context of a satisfactory Cambodia settlement," a lifting of current restrictions should take place after relations are established.

One would hope that the word "reparations" has been struck from the Vietnamese lexicon. Economic assistance of any sort is irrelevant to normalization negotiations—the Russians should not expect the United States to lighten their economic assistance load! On Capitol Hill, foreign aid of any sort is unpopular. In East Asia, it is difficult to arrange even for our friends who need it (the Philippines and Indonesia, for example). For these and other obvious political considerations having to do with memories of the past, the question of U.S. bilateral development assistance does not arise nor is it likely to in the foreseeable future.

There is great potential for private humanitarian assistance to Vietnam, however, and the administration should cooperate in programs devised by U.S. voluntary organizations to help the Vietnamese people, especially religious social-welfare activities. Moreover, official humanitarian programs currently part of the Vessey initiative should be expanded to demonstrate U.S. concern. Sometime in the future, donated food assistance under Public Law 480 should be considered in the context of improving bilateral relations.

Exchanges and people-to-people programs will be extremely important. As soon as relations are established, the administration should propose a menu of cultural, educational, technical, and scientific exchange programs with Vietnam under government and private auspices. A number of pilot programs, exchanges, or one-time visits have already sprung up, even in the absence of normalization. Some of the American organizations already involved are the Social Science Research Council, Georgetown University, the Harvard Institute for International Development, the U.S. Committee for Scientific Exchange, and the Universities of California, Hawaii, Wisconsin, Iowa, Michigan, and Massachusetts, to cite but a few. The United States Information Agency should immediately map out and coordinate a U.S. government-wide plan to stimulate a two-way flow of students, teachers, scientists, journalists, and young leaders. The Asia Foundation, The Asia Society, and similar organizations will automatically become engaged, as will professional groups such as the American Medical Association. This is an area of immense need and potential value in building a new relationship between Vietnam and the United States. In terms of accomplishing long-range U.S. objectives in Indochina, it is "strategic" in the best sense of the word. A few thousand Vietnamese students in the United States and American students in Vietnam would surely promote renovation and "open-mindedness." They could compare notes with the numerous students from the ASEAN countries—and also with the 40,000 Chinese students who are likely to remain in the United States for some time.

9

VIETNAM AND SOUTHEAST ASIA

The United States should look at Vietnam as an integral part of Southeast Asia as well as a potentially valuable country in its own right. In this context, the disastrous condition of the Vietnamese economy, the renewed waves of boat people fleeing to neighboring countries, the relationship of Vietnam with the Soviet Union and with China, and the prospective relationship of Vietnam with ASEAN and with the West are all subjects of concern to U.S. policy as the process of normalization begins.

It is a common saying in Ho Chi Minh City that the lampposts would try to leave Vietnam if they could move—which is a way of underlining that the potential emigration from impoverished Vietnam to the West, and primarily the United States, adds up to millions of people. Nowhere is this more apparent than in the resurgence of refugees from Vietnam in 1988 and even more acutely in 1989, creating a major refugee crisis fourteen years after the first exodus. More than 9,000 Vietnamese arrived in Hong Kong in May 1989 alone and like numbers were expected during the summer's fair weather months. Already bursting at the seams, Hong Kong has instituted a screening process which virtually guarantees that these Vietnamese arrivals will be classified as "economic migrants," not as political refugees eligible for third-country resettlement as was the case after the Vietnam War. Thailand, Indonesia, and Malaysia have adopted stern measures to prevent boat people from landing on their shores. In the case of refugee boats, ships at sea now routinely violate the humanitarian code which dictates that vessels in distress (which the overcrowded Vietnamese boats certainly are) be aided.[1]

From 1975 to 1979 four-fifths of the refugees came from South Vietnam as a direct consequence of the fall of the South Vietnamese regime. Since 1988, however, almost three-quarters of Vietnamese refugees have been from the North, which has lived under communism since 1954. Although Hong Kong is the prime destination for northern boat people during the fair weather season, a similar trend applies to refugees turning up elsewhere in the region. Northerners have braved the high seas and faced Hong Kong detention centers, which are in effect prisons, simply because they are disgusted with a system that has brought economic ruin and offers little hope for improvement. Flight is their only means of expressing discontent.[2]

The Orderly Departure Program in the South has been an ad hoc humanitarian response to a special situation stemming from the war. Hanoi, no doubt, has seen the ODP as a safety valve releasing forces that might otherwise opt for open dissent. In the United States there is already a tight competition for numbers under various quotas—Soviet Jews, Eastern Europeans, refugees from Africa, Afghanistan, and elsewhere. The moral obligations created by the Vietnam War that ended a decade and a half ago seem less compelling. Elsewhere, compassion fatigue has set in, not only in Hong Kong but also to an important extent in most resettlement countries.

At the second International Conference on Refugees in Geneva, June 13–14, 1989, 65 nations met to discuss this situation, which, though different in some respects from the emergency of 1975–79, remains a poignant humanitarian problem involving hundreds of thousands of Indochinese. A six-point "comprehensive plan of action" was adopted that placed emphasis on the Orderly Departure Program and a more direct role for UNHCR. It reasserted the principle of "first asylum," but in formal and informal conference discussions on screening it was evident that only a small percentage of persons fleeing Vietnam will receive refugee status. Thus the question of repatriation, either voluntary or forced, has become central. Remarkably, at one point the United States, the Soviet Union, and Vietnam stood together in opposition to Great Britain and Hong Kong. The conference urged Vietnam to adopt "humane measures" to keep its citizens from leaving the country without permission. Since the conference, there have been reports that Vietnam may accept involuntary repatriation in return for economic assistance from the sending country, for example Hong Kong. While forced repatriation remains abhorrent to Americans and most resettlement countries, it is no longer unthinkable in Hong Kong or in some ASEAN countries, as the conference demonstrated.

Most citizens of Vietnam—be they from the north, center, and south—are depressed economically, as Hanoi's leaders readily admit, and this sad state of affairs results as much from the regime's repression and blunders since 1975 as from the war itself. Normalization and a permanent diplomatic and consular presence in Vietnam, particularly in the South, will bring the United States face-to-face with another level of complexity in this profound humanitarian problem. After establishment of relations, more can be done to assist Vietnamese deserving our support through nongovernmental means and perhaps by the encouragement of privatization.

In the end, the Vietnamese government and the communist party must resolve the country's economic and social problems, which have their roots in two generations of division and conflict. While Hanoi has high-mindedly counseled rapprochement in international relations between former enemies, as yet there is little indication that the party understands the need for genuine reconciliation at home, including respect for their Vietnamese brothers and sisters who fought on the "other side." More than that, as the desperate exodus from the North illustrates, the regime will have to respond to the demands of all its people.

The dimensions of economic change in Vietnam have implications for future U.S. policy and for our friends in the region—Hong Kong, the ASEAN countries, and the international resettlement community. All have an interest in the emergence of a less oppressive regime, politically as well as economically, that offers the Vietnamese people a better standard of living and therefore less reason to flee the country. The question is, do the Vietnamese authorities have the same level of concern?

The signals are mixed. Obviously, the Hanoi leadership would like to escape international opprobrium, but its key policies are driven by different imperatives. The SRV faces the dilemma of other Marxist regimes in the throes of *perestroika*—how to gain economic salvation without losing political control—but with critical differences. Vietnam is decades behind its socialist brethren in economic development and readiness to accept reforms touching the core of Marxism-Leninism. Although it is unclear what long-term impact the spring 1989 turmoil in China will have on Vietnam's own economic reforms, *doi moi* ("renovation") is in its infancy compared with the situation which existed in China up until May 1989. *Coi mo* ("open attitude," roughly equivalent to *glasnost*) is also in its early stages and has already been partly rolled back.[3]

The lingering physical and psychological effects of the war are magnified because the South, having experienced a generation of non-Marxist economic development, is blatantly more prosperous and dynamic than the "victorious" North. Some senior officials, only half in jest, comment to foreigners that today the South is vanquishing the North through its entrepreneurial vitality. The unifying factor of the long "liberation struggle"—the essence of Vietnamese communism's resilience—has disappeared. Since 1975 the people have seen their living standards fall drastically because of the ideological fixation on "socialist transformation" and attendant distortions, benignly described by the party as "mismanagement." The people have little confidence in the system's ability to meet their needs and are openly cynical when asked to make further sacrifices in the name of innovations about which the ruling elite itself seems divided and uncertain.

Since the war, the regime has zigzagged through various economic changes, initially toward centralization, collectivization, eradication of private enterprise, and radical socialist transformation. From 1976 to 1978, the government mounted a precipitous campaign to dismantle the South's free enterprise infrastructure and integrate it with the North's command system, an act roughly analogous to shifting from fourth to first gear in a fast-moving vehicle. The results were predictably disastrous, and Vietnam has been paying the price ever since.

The deteriorating economy was the focus of the Sixth Communist Party Congress in December 1986. Reforms aimed at reducing bureaucratic centralism and stimulating local management and decision-making authority on prices, wages, and production schedules were adopted in principle. A foreign investment code, considered liberal by outside analysts, was also passed. The 1986 Congress was a watershed; it showed the party's readiness to grapple with the need for changes that had been obvious to individual Vietnamese for years. A stream of laws, regulations, and exhortations have since appeared, designed to implement *doi moi.*

Performance has not come close to meeting either the expectations of the communist party or the needs of the people. Some decentralization has taken place; cadre subsidies have been removed or cut; small-scale private enterprise is on the rise, especially in the South; and inflation appears to be decreasing for the time being. But production of food including rice continues to fall behind minimum needs; distribution problems remain as severe as ever; corruption is endemic; and while there has been lively interest by foreign investors, as yet only minor commitments have been made.

The fact that *doi moi* has failed to turn the economy around, and has actually produced some undesirable side effects such as inflation and profiteering, brought on a new crisis in 1989. Within the party and government bureaucracy controversy rages over how fast and far to go in overhauling Marxism-Leninism. Some leaders believe the system that brought victory in war can, with a bit of tinkering, bring prosperity in peace. Others are apparently convinced that far-reaching changes must occur.

But opening up to capitalist economic practices has political dangers. Committed reformers such as Deputy Prime Minister Vo Van Kiet and Vietnamese Communist Party General Secretary Nguyen Van Linh, the chief architects of *doi moi,* are not prepared to see the primacy of the party threatened. Their more conservative colleagues are even more adamant. In response to this latest crisis, the March 1989 Sixth Plenum of the party's

Central Committee, while reaffirming the commitment to *doi moi*, stressed that reforms were designed "not to change the cause of socialism, but to achieve it more quickly." In other words, *doi moi* is an interpretation of Marxism-Leninism that fits current reality and not an abolition of communism. The Plenum unequivocally confirmed the leading role of the party and the concept of the dictatorship of the proletariat.

There has been a parallel cutting back of *coi mo*. Some outspoken newspaper editors have been dismissed; the word has gone out that public criticism must be "constructive." Words like "democracy" have taken on a new meaning: "Broadening democracy in all fields of social life and developing the people's right to mastery is both the goal and the driving force of building socialism. *This is socialist democracy, not bourgeois democracy.* [Emphasis added.] . . . Democracy is applied to the people, but strict punishment must be meted out to those who undermine the gains of the revolution, security, and social order."[4] It seems inevitable that events in China will reinforce the arguments against allowing freer expression in Vietnam, and this in turn is likely to slow down genuine economic reform.

There are implications for U.S. policy here. Can economic liberalization in Vietnam occur without generating accompanying political liberalization? Perhaps the question should be, can economic liberalization occur in the absence of openness in the political realm? The issue is similar to that posed by Gorbachev's *perestroika*, though without the gravity of the U.S.–Soviet relationship or national security ramifications.

The development of Vietnam's external relations will be affected by how *doi moi* unfolds in the context of the classic dilemma of communism confronting economic failure. If Hanoi cannot liberalize the economy without weakening its political grip on Vietnamese society as a whole, particularly the fractious South, it is arguable that the United States should let Vietnam stew in its own Marxist juices and await an explosion that would bring down the system.

This argument is flawed, however, if only because the United States, though influential, is not the sole determinant of

Vietnam's economic future. Moreover, ASEAN would not see chaos in Vietnam desirable for the region as a whole—how many million more Vietnamese would take to the sea? Some ASEAN members, Australia, and several other countries have stated that they will loosen trade and investment restrictions as soon as Vietnam gets its army out of Cambodia. Japan is likely to follow the U.S. lead, but its business community is gearing up to move into the Vietnamese economy as soon as politically feasible. One indicator of the increased interest in Vietnam is the number of international airlines now serving Vietnam. Until a year or two ago, only Air France, Philippine Air Lines, and Thai International (among nonsocialist bloc carriers) flew into Ho Chi Minh City. By the end of 1989, national carriers from Canada, Indonesia, and the Republic of Korea will also serve Vietnam.

A wiser policy would be to move toward diplomatic and economic normalization when issues already on the table—Cambodia and humanitarian concerns—are clearly heading in the right direction from our perspective. The noncommunist world should be able to do business with Vietnamese forces striving for *doi moi,* even with its limitations. While the example of China in recent months is hardly encouraging, the United States should operate on the assumption that, as Marxists correctly fear, political and economic change cannot be separated forever. We should have no illusions, however, that external factors will induce the leadership of Vietnam to adopt measures which could jeopardize their control.

The economic plight of the Vietnamese people will probably have to get much worse before their situation has a chance of getting better. Communist party leaders, through their dogmatism and "mismanagement," have laid the groundwork for change. The evolution of a somewhat more open (one hesitates to use the word "democratic") society responsive to the wishes of the people is desirable from the Western perspective. But how to achieve that sort of society, or anything approaching it, is a job for the Vietnamese people themselves. The government in Hanoi should understand, if there is any doubt on this point, that the United States has no intention of interfering with the internal political or economic affairs of Vietnam. At the same time, it must be apparent that an open relationship will accelerate the process of social change, and this will benefit not only the Vietnamese people but the United States as well. For Hanoi, normalization, like *doi moi,* is not risk-free. From the U.S. perspective, the sooner normalization occurs after a satisfactory Cambodia settlement the better, and indeed normalized relations should promote chances that a settlement will be honored by Vietnam.

THE SOVIET AND CHINESE FACTORS

One strategic objective of U.S. policy should be to encourage a loosening of Vietnam's ties to the Soviet Union. The Soviet presence at Cam Ranh Bay and Danang is dramatic, but not necessarily the most meaningful, evidence of these ties. Cam Ranh Bay and Danang are elaborate, expensive former U.S. installations familiar to many Americans. They improve the Soviets' capability to project military forces not only in the Pacific but into the Indian Ocean, something they could not do nearly as efficiently before 1978. They are superb pieces of military real estate, especially for reconnaissance and surveillance against U.S. forces in the region. Without slighting the value of these "facilities," as they are designated by the Vietnamese, the political and ideological aspects of Soviet-Vietnamese bilateral relations are arguably more significant and durable.

Some military analysts believe Cam Ranh Bay and Danang may be diminishing in practical importance as Moscow tends toward a Pacific "bastion" strategy centered upon existing Soviet capabilities in the Sea of Okhotsk and North Asia generally, rather than the forward deployment of recent years that is expensive operationally and demands a large Soviet Pacific navy. It is not unthinkable that Gorbachev may, at the propitious moment in U.S.–Philippine negotiations, make more precise his offer to relinquish Cam Ranh Bay or even agree to the SRV's "commercialization" of the facilities. (It is quite conceivable that the region's bizarre geopolitics could in the not too distant future find U.S. vessels being painted and taking on fresh water at Cam Ranh—in exchange for hard currency of course.) Having stimulated ASEAN's security concerns by establishing a military presence in the region since 1978, the Soviet Union can reap political gain by reducing that presence.

We should not become excited by the prospect of the Soviets and the Vietnamese quarreling dramatically. Layers of shared interests have been built up through extensive communist party consultations, military-to-military coordination, exchanges, and training in many sectors over twenty years. Vietnam depends on the Soviet Union for virtually all of its military hardware as well as a long list of other essential equipment, technology, and commodities. Westerners cannot judge the depth and sustainability of the ideological bonds between the two regimes, but it would be a mistake to discount Hanoi and Moscow's commitment to preserving the long-term political relationship, in which both have made such large investments. If the alliance can be made more equal for Vietnam and expanded into a wider spectrum of interests, the political relationship stands to be the key element of strength for both countries.

At the same time, this is indisputably a marriage of convenience—in many ways an uncomfortable marriage—with costs as well as benefits to both sides. China is the glue that holds the union together. Hanoi has gotten an insurance policy for the Cambodia adventure and large amounts of Soviet economic and military assistance (between $1 and $2 billion annually) without which it would have collapsed. Moscow has enjoyed military facilities and a strategic position that outflanks China to the south and confronts the United States in the western Pacific. This is a valuable deal for both sides.

As for costs, Vietnam has become economically dependent on and heavily mortgaged to the Soviet Union (which holds most of Vietnam's $8 billion foreign debt). The Soviet presence represents a galling compromise of sovereignty. Russians as people are not well liked by the Vietnamese; whatever ideological fervor exists in the marriage is, as a general rule, not duplicated in personal relations. The Vietnamese are perfectly aware that

Russia's love rests upon politics and geography.[5] The Vietnamese disparage the quality of Soviet assistance and consumer goods that they are forced to buy because of obligatory trade deals. The Soviets are openly critical of Vietnam's squandering of billions in aid over the years, and they have all but commanded Vietnam to put its economic house in order.

Assuming that Soviet rapprochement with China moves ahead, frictions with Vietnam may well mount proportionately, again underlining the differences in national goals: Soviet global considerations as opposed to Vietnam's narrow regional concerns.[6] Despite Soviet reassurances, Vietnam is increasingly concerned over how much the Soviet Union is prepared to pay for better relations with China. In March 1988, the reality of Sino-Soviet rapprochement was well illustrated during the sharp clash with Chinese forces over the disputed Spratly Islands in the South China Sea.[7] Vietnam took casualties and lost several atolls. Much more painful was Moscow's deafening silence—it was two weeks before the Soviets counseled restraint on *both* sides and negotiations. And of course nowhere are the political dimensions of the Soviet-Vietnamese alliance more evident than in Moscow's strong encouragement ("pressure" has not been admitted by either party) to bring the Cambodia issue to the negotiating table and to terminate the Vietnamese occupation.

Despite manifest irritations and some diverging national objectives, ideology and practical needs on both sides bond this marriage of convenience. Any "weaning" of Vietnam (as optimists like to put it) will take years, probably decades, and the United States should not expect an open rupture as occurred in the early days of the Sino-Soviet rift. Moreover, a break in "normal" Soviet-Vietnamese relations need not be a U.S. objective.

Nonetheless there is fertile ground to be plowed once normalization begins.

Vietnamese patriotism and pride remain potent forces. Hanoi knows that Beijing, not Moscow, determines Vietnam's long-term security and that as long as Sino-Vietnamese antagonism remains at a high pitch, its national development will suffer.

Vietnam cannot afford to have either communist superpower decide the fate of Cambodia. Vietnam's vital security interests can be protected best by a solution involving ASEAN and the United States (with Japan, the European Community, and others), and in which international guarantees are present.

Beyond Cambodia and more crucial ultimately, Vietnam must extricate itself from its suffocating reliance on the Soviet Union for protection against China. In the end, Hanoi will have to kow-tow and do what is necessary to reach an accommodation with Beijing. The series of high-level foreign ministry meetings over the past year indicate that Hanoi is prepared to move finally in this direction and that Beijing may eventually find it advantageous to relax some of the pressure if Vietnam in fact removes its army from Cambodia.[8] China will not be kinder or gentler to Vietnam without a price, however, and that price has apparently not yet been agreed upon. Hanoi has been careful in commenting on recent events in China and is no doubt calculating what effects these will have on Chinese external policies.[9]

Multipolarity is the name of one of Vietnam's geopolitical games. Hanoi understands the potential advantages of a more assertive American role in the affairs of Indochina. Acutely aware of its historical vulnerabilities, Vietnam sees the United States as a counterweight to the two other superpowers. A United States presence in Indochina would help Vietnam maneuver against both its current friend, the Soviet Union, and its ancient enemy, China. The United States may face a new and rather peculiar strategic situation. Vietnam's integration into Southeast Asia would tend to dilute Chinese influence. If over time Vietnam becomes economically healthy and closer politically to ASEAN, it would become more independent of the Soviet Union—but it would fear China less. The uncertainty over future directions of Chinese external policies adds spice to the regional geopolitical stew.

The ASEAN countries obviously are key contributors to whatever delicate balancing act Vietnam pursues. All six are deeply suspicious of communism in either its domestic or external expressions, yet simultaneously are pragmatic and confident of their abilities, as individual governments or collectively within ASEAN, to manage whatever risks might arise in a new relationship with Vietnam. Thailand and Indonesia have articulated their desire to see Vietnam as a strong, stable but nonaggressive regional power. It would be a market for ASEAN's wares—and a buffer against China. Stalwartly anticommunist Singapore already enjoys a lively commerce with Vietnam. Thai Prime Minister Chatichai, as noted, is heading full-speed down the commercial track. The Thai baht could become a common currency of the three Indochina countries; Thai banks in Bangkok are poised to do business in Phnom Penh. Indonesia and Malaysia are not far behind.

Vietnam, of course, will try to have it all—close political ties and a security blanket from the Soviets, minimum irritations with China, lucrative trade and aid from Japan and ASEAN, and satisfactory relations with Washington to keep Beijing and Moscow wondering. In this setting, U.S. diplomacy in its own right should be able to maneuver quite nimbly. The potential gains may be relatively minor compared to our interests in North Asia, but one assumption about our geopolitical interest in the region would seem to be incontrovertible: It is not in the strategic interest of the United States for the Soviet Union and China to become the sole architects of Indochina's future political shape or to monopolize Vietnam's political inclinations.

A regional framework for U.S. policy regarding Vietnam must be put in place. Although Vietnam will likely retain a Marxist character for some time, it should be viewed as an integral part of Southeast Asia, as a country with hopes and fears rooted in a long history and a unique culture. The same can be said for Cambodia and Laos. In all three countries of Indochina, given their history and diversity, we might hope for the emergence of some form of national independence away from the communist bloc, and interdependence with ASEAN and other noncommunist trading partners. This trend is already under way between Thailand and Laos, and will be accelerated if and when there is peace in Cambodia. Clearly, it would be naive to dismiss Vietnam's strong historical impulse to ensure an Indochina under its sway, if not hegemony. But national and ethnic antagonisms will persist, and they will influence the policies of individual states despite ideological links and Vietnam's presumed ascendancy in Indochina.

In noncommunist Southeast Asia, economic growth and a more generally shared prosperity are the underpinnings of national political stability and have indeed helped produce peaceful political change in the direction of representative government, for example, in Thailand and to an extent in Indonesia. Similarly, regional prosperity could provide the lure to entice an economically liberated Vietnam from the Soviet embrace. This would take years to accomplish in view of Vietnam's entanglement with COMECON and bilaterally with the Soviets, and because of the glacial pace of any sort of change in the Vietnamese system. At some point ASEAN will probably consider offering Vietnam observer status in the Association. Full membership later would depend in part on Vietnam getting untracked from the communist economic bloc. Formal affiliations aside, the objective would be to engage Vietnam in the life of the region, giving it a stake in stability and an incentive to honor the sovereignty of Cambodia and Laos. This would seem to be a feasible objective.[10]

Riding the tiger has its dangers. ASEAN and the United States would be mistaken to believe that taking the heat off Vietnam as reward for withdrawing its army from Cambodia solves all the problems. For all their ideological fixations, the Vietnamese leaders are learning how to cater to the dreams of mercenary, profit-hungry capitalists. Vietnam is clearly in need of relief from the Cambodia adventure, and it must give top priority to addressing the grave internal problems that have eroded the stature of the communist party. While Vietnam's leaders have made tactical and strategic blunders over the past decades, they have always taken the long view of what they seek to accomplish in the region, using whatever means and whatever allies are available at the moment.

S. Rajaratnam, former Singapore foreign minister, puts it this way: "The Vietnamese, for their part, have no illusions that hit-and-run ASEAN businessmen are the remedy for Vietnam's crippled economy. . . . It would be the height of gullibility to believe that a near bankrupt Vietnam would allow itself to be stripped clean by foreign adventurers. A nation which has astutely milked the Chinese and Soviets for some 30 years will more likely view eager ASEAN businessmen as fat cows to be likewise milked. . . ." Vietnam, Rajaratnam maintains, is using ASEAN business interests "as bait to attract aid and investment from countries that could put Vietnam's combat state back on its economic feet—countries such as the U.S., Japan, Canada, and those of Western Europe."[11] In other words, ASEAN and the United States should not volunteer to rescue Vietnam from the weight of its internal contradictions simply to turn a quick profit—and a relatively small one at that.

These complications recognized, in the post–Cambodia settlement era the United States should encourage the birth of a Vietnam that is reconstructing, developing, and less aggressive—and in the throes of genuine *doi moi* and *coi mo,* which over time could change the basic character of the regime. Were that to come about, Vietnam would still be Vietnam—intensely nationalist and perhaps expansionist, but with an ideology that might be less compulsive.

Friendship and mutual political and economic interests with Thailand, Indonesia, and the other ASEAN states remain central to the United States. This would be true regardless of how dramatically Vietnam was transformed away from Marxism and changed from a tiger to a pussy cat. But the solidarity of ASEAN that we have come to admire so much over the past decade is being severely taxed. There is already a hot debate in ASEAN councils on "what do we do after Cambodia?" and the potential for a resurgence of old national differences. The need for some sort of economic integration, either regionally or in a broader Pacific context, is under intense discussion these days.

However the region evolves, ASEAN's long-term value to the United States now lies more in its successful management of competition and irritations between the member states—that is, maintenance of intra-ASEAN harmony—than in its resistance to

Vietnamese aggression in Cambodia. Whatever happens to ASEAN, the United States must maintain and improve its bilateral relations with each of the six member states individually.

Yet this is precisely why the American perspective on Indochina should be set in a historical framework, plotted in decades or generations not fiscal years. This is not an "either-or" choice. Continued broad, good ties to noncommunist Southeast Asia are not incompatible with developing a new relationship with Vietnam and its smaller Indochina neighbors. The two goals should be complementary. The United States can afford to be imaginative, even a bit daring, as it views Indochina as part of Southeast Asia and broader U.S. objectives in Asia and the Pacific.

The thrust of American strategy in Indochina in the next decade should be to show Vietnam, Cambodia, and Laos that their national interests are served less by Marxism and loyalty to a communist bloc than by peaceful membership in the Southeast Asian community and responsive relations with the West. The region's economic dynamism and steady political evolution in the direction of democracy provide powerful weapons. The United States should work closely with ASEAN and other friends in East Asia to this end.

10

THE PARIS CONFERENCE: STALEMATE OR WORSE?

The International Conference on Cambodia opened in Paris on July 30, 1989, with the foreign ministers of France and Indonesia as co-chairmen, and with UN Secretary General Perez de Cuellar present.[1] In attendance were the five permanent members of the UN Security Council, the six members states of ASEAN, Vietnam, Laos, Japan, India, Australia, Canada, and Zimbabwe (representing the Non-Aligned Movement). The four Khmer Rouge factions, after initial wrangling over the right to represent their country, agreed to jointly occupy the chair for "Cambodia."

The conference established three committees to pursue specific aspects of a comprehensive solution: creation of an international control mechanism to monitor military disengagement and supervise elections; securing Cambodian territorial integrity and neutrality; and repatriation of Cambodian refugees from Thailand and provision of post-settlement reconstruction aid.

The conference sent a fact-finding mission to Cambodia and to Thai border camps under Lieutenant General Martin Vadset, chief of staff of the United Nations Truce and Supervision Organization (UNTSO). The fact that the PRK and Vietnam agreed to this involvement of the United Nations—even though in the context of the Paris conference and not as a formal UN mission—represented a significant change in their position. It seemed to indicate recognition of the need for internationally credible ICM supervision of the Vietnamese withdrawal, which would be a logical follow-on role for UNTSO.

Meanwhile in Paris, while the three formal committees continued their negotiations, the key discussions took place in a fourth, ad hoc, committee made up of the four Cambodian factions and the two conference chairmen. There they struggled with the fundamental issues of power sharing, and particularly the role of the Khmer Rouge, in the transitional arrangements leading to elections. Without agreement on these critical questions, a comprehensive solution would be impossible and any gains in the work of the other committees would be essentially irrelevant. Speaking of Sihanouk's demand for a Khmer Rouge presence in a settlement, Secretary of State Baker had declared in his opening address that, while the United States would accept Sihanouk's judgment, American support for a coalition government would "directly and inversely depend on the extent of Khmer Rouge participation, if any, in that government."

Initial optimism soon gave way to a frustration all too familiar to those acquainted with the Cambodia problem. Intransigence on the part of all four Cambodian factions, as well as their backers, created an impasse in the ad hoc committee. Sihanouk's demands for inclusion of the Khmer Rouge in an interim quadripartite government were met by equally adamant counterdemands by the PRK and Vietnam for exclusion of the Khmer Rouge except on a "council" preparing for elections and overseeing a cease-fire.

On August 30, the conference issued a final communiqué announcing the indefinite suspension of negotiations. Although the meeting had "achieved progress in elaborating a wide variety of elements," the participants concluded it was "not yet possible" to achieve a comprehensive settlement.

The French and Indonesian co-chairmen were to lend their "good offices" to ongoing efforts to reach a comprehensive settlement and were to conduct consultations with the various parties with a view to reconvening the conference in spring 1990. Some conference participants (notably the Vietnamese) predicted an earlier reconvening or at least using the committees as a forum for future talks between the belligerents. Most participants were not so hopeful. A member of Sihanouk's delegation observed that "we are deadlocked here because the military situation is not decisive. If there is no result on the battlefield, there is no result at the negotiating table . . . Hun Sen thinks he can still win the war. That is why he has made no concessions. When he sees he is weak, he will negotiate." Singapore's delegate (his country's ambassador to the United States) observed: "It will be like Afghanistan; there will be more fighting. The two sides are preparing for war, they're already fighting."

Beyond Sihanouk's insistence that the Khmer Rouge be included in a transition government, the Paris conference foundered on several other major issues:

- The precise composition of an international control mechanism;

- the organization of a cease-fire;

- the use of the word "genocide" in describing Cambodia's past history in a final declaration; and

- the future of Vietnamese settlers in Cambodia.

In addition, both China and Sihanouk objected to the use of the term "national reconciliation" in the final communiqué, since their position remained that the Hun Sen government was a "Vietnamese puppet" without authority.

The U.S. chief delegate, Assistant Secretary of State for East Asian and Pacific Affairs Richard Solomon, blamed both of Cambodia's two communist factions for the lack of progress, noting that neither was in a compromising mood and as a result: ". . . if there is no constraint at all, clearly there is a basis for unfettered civil war." Solomon added that the United States opposed such a development even though the unwillingness of the parties to participate in a coalition structure appeared to be forcing events in that direction. At the same time, in the absence of a comprehensive political settlement, the United States opposed creation of an ICM that would lend credibility to the Vietnamese withdrawal.

It was impossible to predict the consequences of the breakdown in Paris. The most hopeful scenario was a return to the stalemate of the past. The worst—but by no means least probable—was outbreak of a full-fledged civil war mainly between the

Khmer Rouge and the PRK. This prospect posed new and extraordinary dangers.

Sihanouk, with limited military force at his disposal, was obliged either to rely on the Khmer Rouge to combat the PRK or to again seek an accommodation with Hun Sen, this time with reduced bargaining power and with less expectation of an acceptable power-sharing arrangement for the noncommunist Khmers. Moreover, the taint of continued close association with the Khmer Rouge threatened to destroy whatever international political clout—and support—Sihanouk still claimed.

For Vietnam and the PRK, increasingly inflexible as the conference proceeded, there were also serious implications. On the surface, they seemed confident of Hun Sen's staying power. But this was far from certain, and there was concern over Vietnamese Foreign Minister Thach's announcement during the conference (echoing the April 5, 1989 Joint Declaration by Vietnam, Laos, and the PRK) that Vietnam retained the right to ". . . reintervene in Cambodia . . . if the Cambodian authorities asked them to come back in." Moreover, having opted for toughing it out (along the lines of the third scenario in Chapter 6), Hanoi now faced an indefinite postponement of normalization of relations with the United States, of the lifting of the economic restrictions by the United States and others, and of attainment of good standing with the international financial institutions.

For Hun Sen, his oft-expressed vow to fight to the bitter end if no political settlement was reached seemed ready to be put to the test, with all the attendant suffering for the Cambodian people and potential political risk to his own control. It remained to be seen if countries like Australia and, most crucially, Thailand would proceed with de facto recognition and increased commerce with the PRK.

For ASEAN, the choice was to return to the policy of economic, political, and insurgency pressure pursued over the past decade or to find some face-saving manner of accepting the PRK's permanence, perhaps by letting the CGDK wither on the vine while finding some other way to attach Sihanouk to the Phnom Penh regime. Yet the problem of what to do with the

Khmer Rouge remained. Continued (let alone expanded) support for the Khmer Rouge in a civil war environment seemed unpalatable to many in ASEAN. As always, the attitude of Thailand was the key, and this was as yet unclear.

The suspension of the Paris conference deepened the policy dilemma of the United States. The risk of placing U.S. hopes so firmly on Sihanouk was glaringly evident. With the negotiating process suspended, the Bush administration again faced the question of increasing its material support for a noncommunist resistance without a coherent political program and whose ability to influence events now lay primarily in military association with the Khmer Rouge in a bloody campaign against fellow Khmers. Morality aside, the domestic political risk of such an investment seemed far greater than any likely profit for U.S. interests on the ground in Cambodia. Yet who was there to place our bets on other than Sihanouk? The alternative seemed to be to adopt a hands-off policy, in effect to let ASEAN—and China— decide the fate of the NCR. Worse yet, there seemed no effective instrument except the Khmer Rouge to unseat Hun Sen or drive him to the bargaining table once more.

Lost in all these calculations, of course, was the fact that whatever social and economic stability seven million Cambodians had managed to achieve since 1979 was now in jeopardy. And their hopes for an end to the killing were again in limbo. Once more the welfare of the Cambodian people seemed to be the least important concern of those forces—communists and noncommunists alike—seeking to shape Cambodia's political future.

NOTES

WHAT'S IN A NAME?

1. See Joseph Buttinger, *The Smaller Dragon: A Political History of Vietnam* (New York: Frederick A. Praeger, Inc., 1958), Chapter 1, "Introducing Vietnam."
2. See MacAlister Brown, "The Indochinese Federation Idea: Learning From History," in Joseph J. Zasloff, ed, *Postwar Indochina: Old Enemies and New Allies* (Washington, D.C.: Foreign Service Institute, Department of State, 1988).

1: INTRODUCTION: VIETNAM AGAIN?

1. Leslie H. Gelb and Richard K. Betts, *The Irony of Vietnam: The System Worked* (Washington, D.C.: The Brookings Institution, 1979), Chapter 2, "Recurrent Patterns and Dilemmas from Roosevelt to Eisenhower," particularly pp. 32–39.
2. See Le Ly Hayslip, *When Heaven and Earth Changed Places: A Vietnamese Woman's Journey from War to Peace* (New York: Doubleday, 1989), for a poignant account of the war's effect upon the Vietnamese people.

2: U.S. INTERESTS IN INDOCHINA

1. For a far-ranging analysis of Gorbachev's Asian policies, see Robert A. Manning, *Asia Policy: The New Soviet Challenge in the Pacific,* A Twentieth Century Fund Paper (New York: Priority Press Publications, 1988).

3: AFTER THE FALL

1. U.S. Congress, House, Committee on International Relations, *The Vietnam-Cambodia Emergency, Part II,* April 1975, p. 244.
2. Press conference May 6, 1975, in *Department of State Bulletin No. 72* (Washington, D.C.: GPO, May 26, 1975), pp. 676–79.
3. Anxious to establish their authority in disputed waters, the Khmer Rouge action could have been directed as much against Vietnam as the United States. See U.S. Congress, House, Committee on International Relations, Subcommittee on International and Political and Military Affairs, *Seizure*

of the Mayaguez, Hearing, Part III, September 12, 1975. See also Roy Rowan, *The Four Days of Mayaguez* (New York: Norton, 1975).

4. "A Pacific Doctrine of Peace With All and Hostility Toward None," address by President Gerald Ford at the University of Hawaii, East-West Center, December 7, 1975, *Department of State Bulletin No. 73* (Washington, D.C.: GPO, December 29, 1975).

5. Henry Kissinger, *White House Years* (Boston: Little, Brown and Company, 1979), p. 223.

6. Henry Kissinger, Japan Society speech, June 18, 1975, *Department of State Bulletin No. 73* (Washington, D.C.: GPO, July 7, 1975), pp. 1–8.

7. U.S. Congress, House, Committee on International Relations, Special Subcommittee on U.S. Policy in Southeast Asia, *Hearings,* September 1976, p. 6.

8. For information on the Trading With the Enemy Act, which authorizes the embargo, see Vladimir N. Pregelj, *U.S. Foreign Trade Sanctions Imposed for Foreign Policy Purposes in Force as of May 31, 1985,* Report 85–781 E (Washington, D.C.: Congressional Research Service, June 18, 1985).

9. Nayan Chanda, *Brother Enemy: The War After the War* (New York: Dodd, Mead and Company, 1986), p. 146, interview with Holbrooke.

10. Cyrus Vance, *Hard Choices: Critical Years in America's Foreign Policy* (New York: Simon and Schuster, 1983), Appendix I, p. 450.

11. Text of the Nixon letter is reproduced in *Congressional Record–House,* June 22, 1977, p. 20920.

12. *The Washington Post,* March 18, 1977, quoted in Chanda, *Brother Enemy, op. cit.,* p. 141.

13. Office of the White House Press Secretary, *Presidential Commission on Americans Missing and Unaccounted for in Southeast Asia: A Report on Trip to Vietnam and Laos, March 16–20, 1977,* Washington, D.C., March 23, 1977, p. 11.

14. President Carter's press conference, March 24, 1977.

15. *Ibid.*

16. U.S. Congress, House, Select Committee on Missing Persons in Southeast Asia, *Final Report Together With Additional and Separate Views of the Select Committee on Missing Persons in Southeast Asia,* Report No. 94–1764, 94th Congress, 2d sess., December 13, 1976, p. 114.

17. Amendment (by Representative John Ashworth) to State Department Authorization Bill for Fiscal Year 1978, Sec. 113. *Congressional Record–House,* May 4, 1977, p. 13417.

18. Amendment (by Senator Robert Dole) to Omnibus Multilateral Development Institutions Act–H.R. 5262, Sec. 703. *Congressional Record–Senate,* May 19, 1977, p. 15625.

19. Chanda, *Brother Enemy, op. cit.,* p. 153.

20. David Truong was the son of Tran Dinh Dzu, a presidential candidate considered "leftist" by RVN President Nguyen Van Thieu and who had been jailed for his political activities some years before.

21. In his summary report to the SRV Council of Ministers on the "Vietnam Volunteer Army's Internationalist Mission in Cambodia," Vice-minister of Defense (concurrently PAVN Chief of Staff) General Doan Khue stated

that during 1977–78 more than 67,000 Vietnamese soldiers and cadres, plus thousands of civilians, were killed or wounded by the Khmer Rouge in cross-border raids. (Hanoi, *Vietnam News Agency*, June 19, 1989, in SRV Permanent Mission to the UN press release no. 15/BC, June 19, 1989.) Khue's report seeks to justify Vietnam's December 1978 intervention and eleven-year occupation of Cambodia. His figures have not been corroborated by U.S. sources.

22. For an exhaustive study of this period see William J. Duiker, *China and Vietnam: The Roots of Conflict* (Berkeley: Institute of East Asian Studies, University of California Press, 1986).

23. Discussion between Hoang and the author in Honolulu, July 12, 1978.

24. Transcript of Phan Hien press conference, referenced in Chanda, *Brother Enemy, op. cit.*, p. 270.

25. See Chanda, *Brother Enemy, op. cit.*, p. 212.

26. John Barron and Anthony Paul, *Murder of a Gentle Land* (New York: Reader's Digest Press, distributed by Thomas Y. Crowell Company, 1977); and François Ponchaud, *Cambodia: Year Zero* (New York: Holt, Rinehart & Winston, 1978). For a limited circulation but brilliant analysis by a political officer at the American embassy in Bangkok during the period, see Timothy M. Carney, *Communist Party Power in Kampuchea (Cambodia)* (Ithaca, N.Y.: Cornell University Southeast Asia Program, Data Paper No. 106, 1977).

27. See William Shawcross, *The Quality of Mercy: Cambodia, Holocaust and Modern Conscience* (New York: Simon and Schuster, 1984), Chapter 7.

28. Vance, *Hard Choices, op. cit.*, p. 123.

4: THE REGIONAL FOCUS

1. For example, see Richard Holbrooke's interview in the *Far Eastern Economic Review*, November 18, 1977, p. 45.

2. Vance, *Hard Choices, op. cit.*, p. 125.

3. *Ibid.*, p. 126.

4. Chanda, *Brother Enemy, op. cit.*, Chapter 10.

5. Vance, *Hard Choices, op. cit.*, pp. 126–27.

6. Elizabeth Becker, *When the War Was Over: The Voices of Cambodia's Revolution and Its People* (New York: Simon and Schuster, 1986), p. 440, from an interview with Brzezinski.

7. Zbigniew Brzezinski, *Power and Principle: Memoirs of the National Security Adviser, 1977–1981* (New York: Farrar Straus Giroux, 1983), p. 207.

8. See Chanda, *Brother Enemy, op. cit.*, Chapter 11.

9. Nayan Chanda, "Support for Sihanouk: U.S. Seeks Hanoi View on Resistance," *Far Eastern Economic Review*, July 14, 1988, p. 13; and Nayan Chanda, "A Lethal Boost: U.S. Shifts Policy to Give Covert Military Aid to Sihanouk," *Far Eastern Economic Review*, October 27, 1988, p. 17.

5: CHANGING TIMES

1. Gerard Hervouet elaborates this theme in *The Return of Vietnam to the International System,* Canadian Institute for International Peace and Security, Occasional Paper No. 6 (Ottawa, 1988).
2. See Manning, *Asia Policy, op. cit.,* Chapter 6.
3. Joint statement carried in *TASS* and *Xinhua,* February 7, 1989.
4. Conversation with the author, July 23, 1988, in Hanoi when Pham Binh was director of the Vietnamese Institute of International Relations.
5. These are consensus figures from the author's discussions with administration officials, journalists, and private analysts.
6. PRK officials to the Council on Foreign Relations study mission, Phnom Penh, March 1989.
7. "Joint Declaration of the Government of the People's Republic of Kampuchea, of the Government of the Lao People's Democratic Republic and of the Government of the Socialist Republic of Vietnam on the total withdrawal of Vietnamese volunteer forces from Kampuchea," contained in SRV Permanent Mission to the UN press release no. 07/BC, April 5, 1989.
8. See Murray Hiebert, "Change in the Air" and "Standing Alone," *Far Eastern Economic Review,* June 29, 1989, pp. 16–18.
9. Steven Erlanger, "Loss of Border Battle to Khmer Rouge Signals Trouble for Cambodian Army," *The New York Times,* August 20, 1989, p. 3.
10. Rodney Tasker and Michael Vatikiotis, "The Prince Offstage," *Far Eastern Economic Review,* August 4, 1988, pp. 13–14; Michael Vatikiotis, "Smiles and Soft Words," *Far Eastern Economic Review,* August 11, 1988, pp. 28–29.
11. United Nations press release GA/7755, November 3, 1988, UN Department of Public Information, New York.
12. Phnom Penh domestic service, May 5, 1989, translated in *Foreign Broadcast Information Service* (East Asia), May 9, 1989.
13. *The New York Times,* May 19, 1989.
14. "Ministers speak at closing," Bandar Seri Begawan radio in English, July 4, 1989, transcribed in *Foreign Broadcast Information Service* (East Asia), July 6, 1989, p. 1.
15. ASEAN press release, "ASEAN foreign ministers call for a comprehensive political settlement of the Kampuchean problem issues in Bandar Seri Begawan," July 3, 1989.

6: END GAME IN CAMBODIA

1. For a masterly historical treatment of Cambodia's travails, see Robert Shaplen, "A Reporter at Large: The Captivity of Cambodia," *The New Yorker,* May 5, 1986.
2. Thach press conference in Hanoi, April 10, 1989, and reiterated in *Washington Post* interview with Elizabeth Becker, September 10, 1989.

3. The ICCS was an attempt to sell the 1973 Paris Peace Accords and rebut the charge of betrayal of the Republic of Vietnam. It soon became a farce that all sides treated contemptuously. It proved useless in deterring the North Vietnamese buildup against the South in 1974–75.

4. "Waiting for the Crunch," *Asia Week,* March 24, 1989.

5. For an in-depth analysis of conditions in Khmer Rouge camps, see "Khmer Rouge Abuses along the Thai-Cambodian Border," *An Asia Watch Report* (Washington, D.C.: Asia Watch, February 1989).

6. For an extended description of life under Khmer Rouge control, see Mary Kay Magistad, "The Khmer Rouge: A Profile," *Indochina Issues,* no. 86, December 1988. See *The Washington Times,* November 11, 1988; *The New York Times,* November 20, 1988; and *The Washington Post,* November 29, 1988, among other news reports.

7. *The Guardian,* London, May 5, 1989. Aid workers see the control of families as a Khmer Rouge method of coercion over its fighters; if a soldier's family is in Khmer Rouge hands, he is less likely to desert.

8. *The Economist,* March 11, 1989, quotes a "well regarded French source" as saying the number of guerrillas sustainable in the field at any one time is no more than 5,000–8,000, depending on the season.

9. Statement of RADM Timothy W. Wright, acting deputy assistant secretary of defense for international security affairs (East Asia and Pacific), before the Subcommittee on Asian and Pacific Affairs, House of Representatives Committee on Foreign Affairs, March 1, 1989.

10. The Thai Army's Task Force 838, an elite, Khmer-speaking special unit, is responsible for monitoring the movement of Cambodian resistance troops in and out of Thailand. See *Asia Week,* March 24, 1989.

11. After translation from the original Khmer language and careful study by the intelligence community, this document has been accepted as authentic. For a fuller account, see Magistad, *Indochina Issues,* no. 86, *op. cit.*

12. See Amnesty International's report, "Kampuchea: Political Imprisonment and Torture" (New York: Amnesty International Publications, June 1987).

13. The summary assessment in these paragraphs is based upon the author's visits in August 1988 and (with the Council on Foreign Relations study mission) March 1989 to Cambodia and Vietnam where he had interviews with PRK officials, foreign diplomats, journalists, and voluntary agency personnel. It is also informed by articles in the *Far Eastern Economic Review* and *Asia Week,* among other journals and newspapers.

14. See also Murray Hiebert, "Rising from the Ashes," *Far Eastern Economic Review,* January 12, 1989; and Susan Blaustein, "Cambodia's Future: Looking to the Private Sector," *The Nation,* February 20, 1989.

15. For opposing views of the PRK and Hun Sen, see Elizabeth Becker, "Vietnam's Gift to Cambodia," *The New York Times,* April 11, 1989, and Lally Weymouth, "Cambodia's Hun Sen Is No Savior," *The Washington Post,* April 16, 1989.

16. As Hun Sen observed to the Council on Foreign Relations study mission, March 8, 1989, "We do not pay much attention to whether we are following socialist reconstruction of the economy or not but, rather, how to put an

end to the poverty of the people. What we fear is not private enterprise but the continued poverty of the population."

17. *Foreign Broadcast Information Service* (Southeast Asia), March 24, 1989, quoting Phnom Penh radio.
18. "See Steven Erlanger, "In Cambodia, Calls to Resist the Khmer Rouge," *The New York Times,* August 27, 1989, p. 13.
19. Sources for this conclusion are western voluntary agency representatives interviewed in Phnom Penh, and discussions with retired British diplomat John Pedler, who spent ten days traveling extensively in the provinces in 1988. See his "Cambodia: Danger and Opportunity for the West," *The World Today* (London: The Royal Institute of International Affairs, February 1989).
20. Wright testimony, House Foreign Affairs Subcommittee on Asian and Pacific Affairs, March 1, 1989.
21. *Ibid.*
22. See "Thailand-Cambodia: Major Issues of U.S. Policy in East Asia," staff report of the Committee on Foreign Relations, United States Senate (Washington, D.C.: GPO, March 1989).
23. Testimony of David Lambertson, deputy assistant secretary of state for East Asian and Pacific Affairs, before the House Foreign Affairs Subcommittee on Asian and Pacific Affairs, March 1, 1989.
24. Stephen J. Solarz, "Pol Pot Could Return," *The Washington Post,* April 19, 1989.
25. Vice President Quayle's speech before The Heritage Foundation Asian Studies Center "Conference on U.S. Policy in Asia: Challenges for 1990," Washington, D.C., June 22, 1989.

7: CHALLENGES FOR U.S. POLICY

1. Vice President Quayle at the Heritage Foundation, June 22, 1989, *op. cit.*
2. See "Preventing the Return of the Khmer Rouge," *F.A.S. Public Interest Report,* Journal of the Federation of American Scientists, vol. 42, no. 4 (April 1989), for a collection of articles, interviews with PRK personnel, and opinion pieces critical of U.S. policy.
3. Testimony of Cambodian-American leaders Than Pok and Vora Huy Kanthoul, before a hearing of the House Foreign Affairs Subcommittee on Asian and Pacific Affairs, chaired by Representative Solarz, March 1, 1989.
4. S. 928, State Department Authorization Bill, 100th Congress, Title VIII–Policy Provisions: Sec. 801. "Policy on Cambodia," May 4, 1989.
5. Don Oberdorfer, "China Offers Asylum for Pol Pot," *The Washington Post,* June 18, 1988. See also Reuters report from Bangkok, June 23, 1988, in which Beijing denied that such an offer had been made.
6. See Steven Erlanger, "700 Refugees to Be Returned to Khmer Rouge," *The New York Times,* June 26, 1989, p. A1.
7. Soviet news agency TASS, February 5, 1989, in a Soviet embassy press release, Washington, D.C., February 6, 1989.

8. Author's interviews with UN officials, September 1988 and April 1989.
9. For example see Youssef M. Ibrahim, "Talks Among Cambodian Factions Break Off in Dismay in France," *The New York Times,* July 16, 1989, p. A2.

8: THE STRANGE COLD WARMTH OF NORMALIZATION

1. Vice President Quayle's speech before the Heritage Foundation, June 22, 1989, *op. cit.,* is a recent reiteration. See also Lambertson testimony before the House Foreign Affairs Subcommittee on Asian and Pacific Affairs, March 1, 1989, *op. cit.*
2. *Ibid.*
3. A senior U.S. official, speaking of the Vessey visit, said bluntly, "This means we crossed a line we never crossed before . . . " Quoted in *The New York Times,* September 6, 1987.
4. Data from the Department of Defense, Office of the Assistant Secretary of Defense for International Security Affairs, East Asia and Pacific Region, and from the Department of State, East Asia and Pacific Bureau.
5. Data from the Department of State, Bureau of Refugee Affairs.
6. Foreign Minister Thach cites, among other incidents, the July 1987 incursion from Thailand (through the Lao panhandle) into Vietnam by former RVN Admiral Hoang Co Minh and a reported 200 guerrillas, of whom Hanoi claimed to have killed 104 and captured 65. The survivors were eventually tried; all but a few were executed for treason. Peter Eng, "Vietnam Rebels Face Trial," *Associated Press,* Bangkok, November 30, 1987; "Trial of Counter-Revolutionaries Open," *Hanoi Domestic Service* in Vietnamese, December 1, 1987, translated in *Foreign Broadcast Information Service* (East Asia), December 1, 1987, p. 49.
7. Doan Van Toai, a prominent writer whose works include *The Vietnamese Gulag* describing life under communism, was a recent victim. Toai, who has expressed support for normalization, was shot by unknown assailants on August 19, 1989, in Fresno, California.

9: VIETNAM AND SOUTHEAST ASIA

1. Henry Kamm, "All the World Stands Ready To Turn Away the Boat People," *The New York Times,* June 25, 1989, p. E3.
2. Keith B. Richburg, "Asia's Tide of Protest," *The Washington Post,* June 25, 1989, p. B1.
3. Economic reform in Vietnam has been the subject of numerous media articles and scholarly studies over the past three years. See for example: "Vietnam—Slow Progress," *Far Eastern Economic Review,* March 17, 1988; Huynh Kim Khanh, "Vietnam's Reforms: 'Renewal or Death,'" *Indochina Issues,* no. 84, September 1988; Len Ackland, "Vietnam: Unified, Inde-

pendent and Poor," *Editorial Research Reports* (Washington, D.C.: Congressional Quarterly, vol. 1, no. 11, March 18, 1988); Douglas Pike, "The Year 1988 in Vietnam: Promises, Promises," *Yearbook on International Communist Affairs* (Stanford, Cal: Hoover Institution, January 1, 1989); Lewis M. Stern, "Economic Change and Party Reform in Vietnam, 1987," *Asian Affairs,* Spring 1988; and Stern's "Nguyen Van Linh's Leadership: A New Operational Code," *Indochina Report,* no. 18 (January–March 1989).

4. *Hanoi Domestic Service,* March 31, 1989, translated in *Foreign Broadcast Information Service* (East Asia), as excerpted in Lewis M. Stern, "The Sixth Plenary Session of the Vietnamese Communist Party's Central Committee, 20–29 March 1989," unpublished paper for the Aspen Institute Indochina Policy Forum, Washington, D.C., May 22, 1989.

5. This judgment rests on the author's discussions with Vietnamese officials and foreign observers in Hanoi and elsewhere in Vietnam.

6. See Manning, *op. cit.;* Charles McGregor, "The Sino-Vietnamese Relationship and the Soviet Union," *Adelphi Papers,* 232 (London: The International Institute for Strategic Studies, Autumn 1988); and Douglas Pike, *Vietnam and the USSR* (Boulder, Colo.: Westview Press, 1986).

7. Jerry Cushing, "Beached Again on the Shoals," *Far Eastern Economic Review,* March 17, 1988, p.23.

8. See Nayan Chanda, "Taking a soft line: Vietnam signals China that it wants improved relations," *Far Eastern Economic Review,* December 8, 1988.

9. For example, *Vietnam News Agency,* Hanoi, June 7, 1989, in which Foreign Minister Thach, when asked about events in China over the preceding days, was quoted as saying, "This is an internal question of China. The bloodshed is regrettable. It is hoped that the situation in China will soon return to normal."

10. See for example interview with Thai Deputy Foreign Minister Praphat Limpaphan after a visit to Vietnam, carried in *The Nation,* April 28, 1989, transcribed in *Foreign Broadcast Information Service* (East Asia), May 4, 1989, p. 54. See also Nguyen Co Thach's address to a Bangkok conference on Indochina trade, "Turning a War Zone into a Trade Zone," *Hanoi Domestic Service* in Vietnamese, translated in *Foreign Broadcast Information Service* (East Asia), April 29, 1989, p. 4.

11. S. Rajaratnam, "Riding the Vietnamese Tiger," *Far Eastern Economic Review,* May 4, 1989, p. 20. Singapore businessmen have conducted a lively commerce with Vietnam and Cambodia in recent years, and the Singapore government has advocated "plugging Vietnam into the Western economic grid" as a means of taming the Vietnamese tiger.

10: THE PARIS CONFERENCE: STALEMATE OR WORSE?

1. Sources in this chapter are *The New York Times, The Washington Post, The Washington Times,* Associated Press, United Press International, and *Foreign Information Broadcast Service* reporting of French and Asian media during the period August 1–30, 1989.

FOR FURTHER READING

Books about Indochina are being published at an astonishing rate—histories, memoirs, biographies, novels, poetry, scholarly analyses of why we and our South Vietnamese allies lost. Many of the histories were written years ago by Robert Shaplen, Bernard Fall, Ellen Hammer, Joseph Buttinger, Lucien Bodard, Jules Roy, David Marr, Jeffrey Race. To this list we can add newer works by Nayan Chanda, Neil Sheehan, and Stanley Karnow. In the 1960s, U.S. civilians preparing to work in the Vietnamese provinces were told they needed to read only two books to understand the war: Graham Greene's *The Quiet American* and Lewis Carroll's *Alice in Wonderland*. What follows is not intended as a definitive bibliography. Included are works of relevance to the themes of the present book, plus classics for anyone who seeks to understand the past and hopes for better relations between the United States and the three countries of Indochina in the future.

HISTORY AND ANALYSIS

Bodard, Lucien. *The Quicksand War: Prelude to Vietnam*. Boston: Little, Brown and Company, 1963.

Braestrup, Peter. *Big Story: How the American Press and Television Reported and Interpreted the Crisis of Tet 1968 in Vietnam and Washington*. 2 vols. Boulder, Colorado: Westview Press, 1977.

Buttinger, Joseph. *The Smaller Dragon: A Political History of Vietnam*. New York: Praeger, 1958.

Chanda, Nayan. *Brother Enemy: The War After the War*. New York: Harcourt Brace Jovanovich, 1986.

Cooper, Chester L. *The Lost Crusade: America in Vietnam*. New York: Dodd, Mead and Company, 1970.

Duiker, William J. *China and Vietnam: The Roots of Conflict.* Berkeley, California: Institute of East Asian Studies, University of California, 1986.

Emerson, Gloria. *Winners & Losers.* New York: Random House, 1972.

Fall, Bernard. *Hell in a Very Small Place: The Siege of Dien Bien Phu.* Philadelphia: J.B. Lippincott Company, 1966.

————. *Street Without Joy.* Harrisburg, Pennsylvania: The Stackpole Company, 1965.

————. *The Two Viet-Nams: A Political and Military Analysis.* New York: Praeger, 1963.

FitzGerald, Frances. *Fire in the Lake.* Boston: Little, Brown and Company, 1972.

Gelb, Leslie H. and Richard K. Betts. *The Irony of Vietnam: The System Worked.* Washington, D.C.: The Brookings Institution, 1979.

The Senator Gravel Edition, *The Pentagon Papers.* 4 vols. Boston: Beacon Press, 1971.

Hammer, Ellen J. *A Death in November: America in Vietnam, 1963.* New York: E.P. Dutton, 1987.

————. *The Struggle for Indochina, 1940–1955.* Stanford, California: Stanford University Press, 1954.

Hannah, Norman B. *The Key to Failure: Laos & the Vietnam War.* Lanham, Maryland: Madison Books, 1987.

Hung, Nguyen Tien and Jerrold L. Schecter. *The Palace File.* New York: Harper & Row, 1986.

Isaacs, Arnold. *Without Honor: Defeat in Vietnam and Cambodia.* New York: Vintage Books, 1984.

Karnow, Stanley. *Vietnam: A History. The First Complete Account of Vietnam at War.* New York: Viking Press, 1983.

Lacouture, Jean. *Ho Chi Minh: A Political Biography.* New York: Vintage Books, 1968.

Lewy, Guenter. *America in Vietnam.* New York: Oxford University Press, 1978.

Manning, Robert, editor-in-chief. *The Vietnam Experience.* A 16-volume series on the American experience in Vietnam. Boston: Boston Publishing Company, 1984.

Marr, David. *Vietnamese Anticolonialism, 1885–1925.* Berkeley, California: University of California Press, 1971.

McAlister, John T., Jr., and Paul Mus. *The Vietnamese and Their Revolution.* New York: Harper & Row, 1970.

Race, Jeffrey. *War Comes to Long An: Revolutionary Conflict in a Vietnamese Province.* Berkeley, California: University of California Press, 1972.

Roy, Jules. *The Battle of Dienbienphu.* New York: Pyramid Books, 1965.

Rust, William J. *Kennedy in Vietnam: American Vietnam Policy 1960–1963.* New York: Charles Scribner's Sons, 1985.

Schandler, Herbert Y. *The Unmaking of a President: Lyndon Johnson and Vietnam.* Princeton: Princeton University Press, 1977.

Shaplen, Robert. *The Lost Revolution.* New York: Harper & Row, 1965.

Sheehan, Neil. *A Bright Shining Lie: John Paul Vann and America in Vietnam.* New York: Random House, 1988.

Smith, Ralph. *Vietnam and the West.* Ithaca, New York: Cornell University Press, 1971.

Toai, Doan Van and David Chanoff. *The Vietnamese Gulag.* New York: Simon and Schuster, 1986.

Warner, Dennis. *Certain Victory: How Hanoi Won the War.* Kansas City: Sheed Andrews and McMeel, 1977.

Zasloff, Joseph J., ed. *Postwar Indochina: Old Enemies and New Allies.* Washington, D.C.: Foreign Service Institute, U.S. Department of State, 1988.

MEMOIRS

Broyles, William, Jr. *Brothers in Arms: A Journey From War to Peace.* New York: Alfred A. Knopf, 1986.

Diem, Bui, and David Chanoff. *In the Jaws of History.* Boston: Houghton Mifflin Co., 1987.

Don, Tran Van. *Our Endless War.* San Rafael, California: Presidio Press, 1978.

Dung, General Van Tien. *Great Spring Victory.* Series carried in *Nhan Dan* newspaper, Hanoi, SRV, beginning April 1, 1976. Translated from Vietnamese in *Foreign Broadcast Information Service* supplements, FBIS-APA-76-110, June 7, 1976, and FBIS-APA-76-131, July 7, 1976.

Glasser, Ronald J., M.D. *365 Days.* New York: George Braziller, 1971.

Hosmer, Stephen T., Konrad Kellen, Brian M. Jenkins. *The Fall of South Vietnam: Statements by Vietnamese Military and Civilian*

Leaders. R-2208-OSD (HIST). Santa Monica: The Rand Corporation, 1978.

Le Ly Hayslip. *When Heaven and Earth Changed Places.* New York: Doubleday, 1989.

Parrish, John A., M.D. *12, 20 & 5: A Doctor's Year in Vietnam.* New York: E.P. Dutton, 1972.

Santoli, Al. *To Bear Any Burden.* New York: E.P. Dutton, 1985.

Sheehan, Susan. *Ten Vietnamese.* New York: Alfred A. Knopf, 1967.

Snepp, Frank. *Decent Interval.* New York: Random House, 1977.

CAMBODIA

Barron, John, and Anthony Paul. *Murder of a Gentle Land.* New York: Reader's Digest Press, 1977.

Becker, Elizabeth. *When the War Was Over: The Voices of Cambodia's Revolution and Its People.* New York: Simon and Schuster, 1986.

Carney, Timothy M. *Communist Party Power in Kampuchea (Cambodia).* Data Paper No. 106. Ithaca: Cornell University Southeast Asia Program, 1977.

Chandler, David P. *A History of Cambodia.* Boulder, Colorado: Westview Press, 1983.

Criddle, Joan D., and Teedabutt Man. *To Destroy You Is No Loss: The Odyssey of a Cambodian Family.* New York: The Atlantic Monthly Press, 1987.

Haing Ngor (with Roger Warner). *A Cambodian Odyssey.* New York: Macmillan Company, 1987.

May, Someth. *Cambodian Witness: The Autobiography of Someth May.* Edited by James Fenton. London: Faber and Faber, 1986.

Ponchaud, François. *Cambodia: Year Zero.* New York: Holt, Rinehart & Winston, 1978.

Shawcross, William. *The Quality of Mercy: Cambodia, Holocaust and Modern Conscience.* New York: Simon and Schuster, 1984.

————. *Sideshow: Kissinger, Nixon and the Destruction of Cambodia.* New York: Simon and Schuster, 1979.

Sihanouk, Norodom. *My War With the CIA.* As related to William Burchett. New York: Pantheon Books, 1972.

Szymusiak, Molyda. *The Stones Cry Out: A Cambodian Childhood, 1975–1980.* New York: Hill and Wang, 1986.

FICTION

Bunting, Josiah. *The Lionheads.* New York: Popular Library, 1972.

Downs, Frederick. *The Killing Zone: My Life in the Vietnam War.* New York: W.W. Norton, 1978.

Greene, Graham. *The Quiet American.* New York: The Viking Press, 1956.

Lomperis, Timothy. *Reading the Wind: The Literature of the Vietnam War.* Durham, North Carolina: The Duke University Press (for the Asia Society), 1987.

O'Brien, Tim. *Going After Cacciato.* New York: Dell Publishing Co., 1975.

Webb, James. *Fields of Fire.* Englewood Cliffs, New Jersey: Prentice-Hall, 1978.

GLOSSARY OF
ABBREVIATIONS AND ACRONYMS

ANS	Armee Nationale Sihanoukiste
ASEAN	Association of Southeast Asian Nations
CGDK	Coalition Government of Democratic Kampuchea
COMECON	Council for Mutual Economic Assistance
DK	Democratic Kampuchea
EC	European Community
FUNCINPEC	Front Uni National Pour un Cambodge Independent, Neutre, Pacifique et Cooperatif
ICC	International Control Commission
ICCS	International Commission of Control and Supervision
ICK	International Conference on Kampuchea
ICM	International Control Mechanism
ICRC	International Committee of the Red Cross
IPKF	International peacekeeping force
JIM	Jakarta Informal Meeting
KNUFNS	Kampuchean National United Front for National Salvation
KPNLAF	Khmer People's National Liberation Armed Forces
KPNLF	Khmer People's National Liberation Front
KPRAF	Kampuchean People's Revolutionary Armed Forces
KPRP	Kampuchean People's Revolutionary Party
KUFNCD	Kampuchean United Front for National Construction and Defense
LPDR	Lao People's Democratic Republic
MIA	Missing in action

MOULINAKA	Mouvement Pour la Liberation Nationale de Kampuchea
NADK	National Army of Democratic Kampuchea
NCR	Noncommunist resistance
NIE	Newly industrializing economy
NSC	National Security Council
OPP	Orderly Departure Program
PAVN	People's Army of Vietnam
POW	Prisoner of war
PRC	People's Republic of China
PRK	People's Republic of Kampuchea
RVN	Republic of Vietnam
SEANWFZ	Southeast Asia Nuclear Weapons–Free Zone
SOC	State of Cambodia
SRV	Socialist Republic of Vietnam
UN	United Nations
UNBRO	United Nations Border Relief Organization
UNDP	United Nations Development Programme
UNHCR	United Nations High Commissioner for Refugees
UNTSO	United Nations Truce and Supervision Organization
USIA	United States Information Agency
USSR	Union of Soviet Socialist Republics
ZOPFAN	Zone of Peace, Freedom, and Neutrality

APPENDIX

Council on Foreign Relations Study Group
"Indochina: Looking Beyond 1990"

Julia Chang Bloch—Harvard University
Stephen W. Bosworth—U.S.–Japan Foundation
Marshall M. Bouton—The Asia Society
Karen McConnell Brooks—University of Minnesota
Frederick Z. Brown—Consultant
Nayan Chanda—*Far Eastern Economic Review*
Evelyn Colbert—Johns Hopkins School of Advanced International Studies
William H. Gleysteen, Jr.—Council on Foreign Relations
Jamie Gough—Council on Foreign Relations
Rita E. Hauser—Stroock & Stroock & Lavan
Nguyen Manh Hung—George Mason University Indochina Institute
Amos A. Jordan—Center for Strategic and International Studies
David Lambertson—U.S. Department of State
Richard A. Melville—Investment Advisor
Margaret Osmer-McQuade—Council on Foreign Relations
Maynard Parker—*Newsweek*
Alan D. Romberg—Council on Foreign Relations
Edward G. Sanders—IPAC, Inc.
Sichan Siv—International Institute of Education
Stephen J. Solarz—U.S. House of Representatives
Richard Stillwell—U.S. Army (Retired)
Peter Tarnoff—Council on Foreign Relations
Cyrus R. Vance—Simpson, Thacher & Bartlett
John W. Vessey, Jr.—U.S. Army (Retired)
Stephen B. Young—Winthrop & Weinstine

INDEX

ABOUT THE AUTHOR

Frederick Z. Brown was a foreign service officer from 1958–84, with assignments in France, Thailand, the Soviet Union, and Cyprus. He served twice in Vietnam as a provincial advisor in Vinh Long (1968–70) and as consul general in Danang (1971–73), and worked on Southeast Asian affairs in Washington as country director for Vietnam, Laos, and Cambodia (1977–78) and as country director for Indonesia, Malaysia, Burma, and Singapore (1980–83). Mr. Brown was a professional staff member for East Asia and the Pacific on the Senate Foreign Relations Committee (1984–87). Most recently he was a senior associate at the Carnegie Endowment for International Peace.